MW01670661

To: Bill

Thanks for the support.
Treasures are found in places
that are often overlooked

... in the heart,
in the soul,

and

Write Under Your Nose

Best Wishes
[signature]
6/03

# WRITE UNDER YOUR NOSE

# WRITE UNDER YOUR NOSE



Sheridan – 2003

ISBN:
0-9708748-9-8

COVER DESIGN by Michael Lewis
OIL PAINTINGS by Shanda Murff
BOOK DESIGN by Robin Perry
BOOK PHOTOGRAGHY by Chris Cozzone
EDITED by Kimberly McNeil

PRINTED IN THE U.S.A.

# DEDICATION PAGE

**To my Uncle Dumpy**
**Eugene Dickerson, Jr.**
A great man
who found God
while serving time;
who loves his family
and converted his life
to Christianity

**To my brother-in-law**
**Donovan Bell**
A strong man
who lost his youth
in the system.
His body remains
temporarily captive
but his love for God and family
has no bounds.

**To everyone serving time**
This is for you.
You are important.
You are talented.
You are skilled.
You are loved.
And most importantly,
You are never forgotten.

Be inspired to make the best out of your situation.

If you can't be the best,
DO YOUR BEST!

# ACKNOWLEDGEMENTS:

*Johnice Dickerson (my wife) and Jhane' Dickerson (my daughter)* – thanks for supporting and believing in me. There is nothing more valuable than the welcomed love of your family.

*The Vaughn family and The Dickerson family* – thanks for being the village that raised me and for instilling the principles of trusting and believing in God because through Him all things are possible. I love you.

*Michael Lewis (artist)* – thanks for being a part of this book project. I have always considered you to be an extraordinary talented artist and poet. I look forward to our next project.

*Shanda Murff (painter)* – thanks for providing limited edition oil paintings for this project.

*Dr. Loren Blanchard (mentor)* – thanks for giving me the initial inspiration to do this. Being my big brother and mentor in life has always influenced me to strive for more.

*Robin Perry (project coordinator)* – thanks for seeing this project through. My brother, you are a superlative executive director and friend.

*Damien Mitchell, Eric "Scooter" Ross, Larry Lewis, and Kimberly McNeil (support staff)* – thanks for being the backbone of this project with hours of dedication and revelations.

*Angel, Serena, Armond, and Earl (models)* – thanks for being accommodating and quite photogenic. Your real beauty is within but it is nice to know that it also radiates outward.

*Tawana Jones (typist)* – thanks for being there on the forefront and building the structure of the book. You are indeed well organized and thorough. Your participation has truly been value-added.

*Wardens and Prison Ministries* – thanks for being receptive to this project and the fair and impartial treatment of the inmates. Your involvement was critical and truly appreciated.

# CONTENT

# PREFACE

The obstacles have been many but the rewards have been great in compiling the works for this book. This project has given me the opportunity to speak for those whose voice has been taken away and to empower just a few of the many gifted inmates who are serving time.

My uncle, Eugene Dickerson Jr., a good man I affectionately call, "Uncle Dumpy," provided the inspiration for this compilation several years ago. While attending church service together, Uncle Dumpy stood up to give his testimony. At his conclusion he recited a very moving poem. When he finished, I asked him who had written the poem. When he replied that he was the author, I was stunned. I was aware that my uncle had served eight years in the penitentiary, that he had turned his life around and accepted God into his life, but I never realized that he possessed such a unique gift. He opened my eyes to the countless inmates who spend years cultivating their talents and never get the chance to share one word with anyone outside of those prison walls.

*Write Under Your Nose* serves as a platform for some of the writers and artists who would otherwise never publish their work or have their talent recognized. More importantly, it serves as an incentive for other inmates to undertake writing for the first time, to tell their story, to share their unusual perspective with society. The other objective of this project is to provide a therapeutic diversion from other potentially harmful activities, to offer relief from the boredom and a possible aid in rehabilitation.

I hope you are able to feel the sincerity expressed through the words of these authors: the brothers, husbands, fathers, uncles, sisters, mothers, cousins, etc. absent but not forgotten by their family and friends. I hope you allow yourself to glimpse at life through their eyes and experience a perspective different than the mass media's flat portrayal of the men and women merely referred to as "inmates." Take a few minutes to appreciate the talent that is *Write Under Your Nose*.

Learnard Gene Dickerson

# Spirituality

**I will lead the blind by ways they have not known, along unfamiliar paths I will guide them; I will turn the darkness into light before them and make the rough places smooth. These are the things I will do; I will not forsake them.** *Isaiah 42:16*

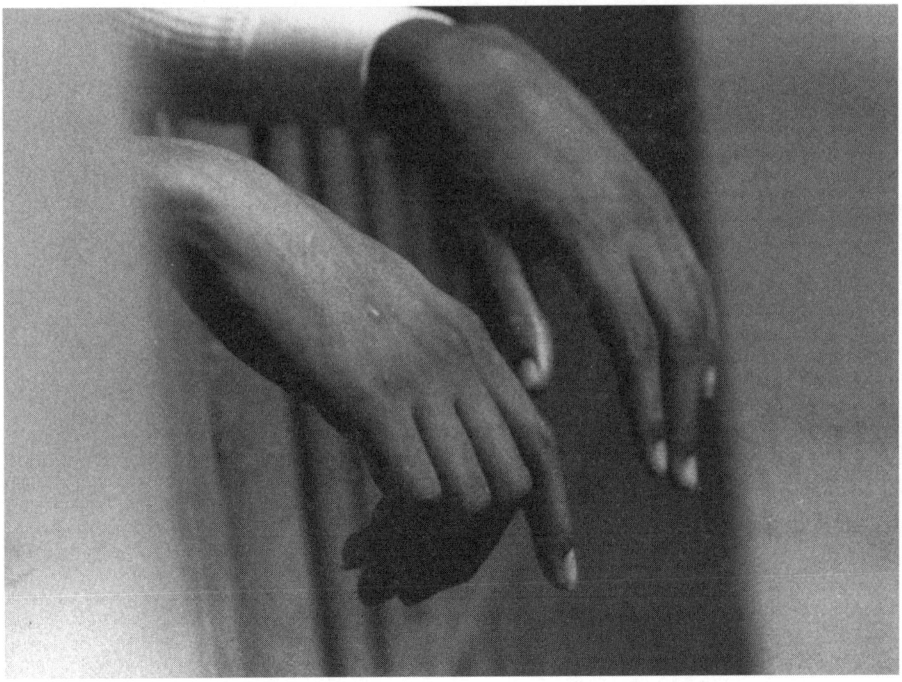

## THE FEATHER

By: Steven J. Anderson

Drifting lazily upon the wind,
A message perhaps, that God did send.
Gently floating it begins to fall.
Its' meaning unique, not same to all.

A single, white feather, so downy soft,
with a gust of wind it stays aloft.
Slowly settling upon the ground,
a destiny awaits when it is found.

A young girl walks, her eyes with tears,
now she faces her greatest fears.
He loved her, he said upon the phone.
But now with child, she's left alone.

What to do: keep it or not?
The choice is hers, is what she thought.
But this life inside now has a say.
This young girl's life has changed today.

Abort it now and life goes on.
Chessboard of life and she's the pawn.
Or keep this child, it occurs,
because it's now a part of her.

The tears now flow as she bitterly cries.
What she believed has turned to lies.
She prays to God to take her life,
as she holds the handle of the knife.

Her decision made, she whispers goodbye.
Then something white catches her eye,
a single white feather – a memory dim,
an older brother, she laughs with him.

A night of laughter as they rolled about,
a crazy time, they scream and shout.
Tears of joy from each other,
while feather-tickled by their mother.

From this memory two lives live.
To her child, now this she'll give,
a joy for life, and shall be seen,
what was a pawn becomes a queen.

It floats once more upon the wind,
a wordless message that God did send,
to intertwine into a life,
that's torn apart by internal strife.

The young wife sat beside his bed,
a tumor growing inside his head.
One hope he has, they tell them.
But the chances of living are very slim.

He wiped away her flowing tears.
Tried his best to ease her fears.
"You must have faith, believe in God."
Her only answer a silent nod.

"Faith is like a feather, you see.
One won't do it, nor will three.
It takes a bunch for birds to fly.
With faith in God I will not die."

She decided to go for a walk,
to be alone, to God she'd talk,
"God," she cried, "let him live.
Whatever it takes I will give!"

A breeze sprung up and from the sky.
A single, white feather came floating by.
The answer God gave was very clear:
"With faith in Me, there is not fear."

A feeling came, a peace she found,
as she picked it up from the ground.
Feather in hand, she walked on back.
A faith in God, she'd never lack.

The doctor smiled as she came inside.
"Everything's fine," he said with pride.
Dropping the feather as she wept with joy,
later to be found by a sad little boy.

It's funny how when you least expect,
you're filled once more with awe and respect,
for all the wonders that God can do,
when all it takes is faith from you.

"Your mama is gone," wept the dad.
"We must be strong and not be mad."
"Where has she gone?" the young boy cried.
"To live with the angels," his father sighed.

In grief-stricken misery, he began to cry.
With tears in eyes, looked to the sky.
"Mama, will you have those halo things?
A long, white dress and pretty, white wings?"

"Will you be able to listen, be able to talk?
Go outside and take a walk?
Mama, I'll miss you, can't you see?
Please, come back, don't leave me!"

His father wept, lost in sorrow,
too tired to go on, to face tomorrow,
as the young boy cried more than before.
Until, suddenly, he saw it upon the floor.

Slowly a smile, then happiness flowed.
A single, white feather to him that showed,
his mama had left but was now back here.
An angel's feather - she was very near.

Grabbing the feather, he ran to his dad,
"Mama is back, so don't be sad."
Into his face the father gazed.
Thought of God's love and was totally amazed.

Together they walked out through the doors,
not feeling alone as just before.
As they turned down the walk, you could barely see,
that instead of two, it now was three.

A single, white feather floats in the wind.
A message perhaps, that God did send.
His breath is wind and it's in the air.
Our lives can be guided through faith and prayer.

Sometimes we may stumble, trip and fall,
but He'll always be waiting, just give him a call.
We are never alone for He's always above,
gazing upon us with all His love.

## JUDGEMENT DAY

By: Sharon White

PRIEST: My child, do you ever feel remorse? How long has it been?
CHILD: What is remorse, Father? Is it when . . .

You've grown up despised by your older sibling because you're the youngest and a girl?
Being sheltered and protected, never told of the elements of this world?

Getting pregnant at sixteen, could have had the world at your feet?
Three days before your wedding, your fiancé dies in a skip of a beat?

Your best friend gets killed just hours after talking to you on the phone?
To come home one day and find your father just died in your home?

You're charged with manslaughter, you're on your way upstate?
Feeling everyday of your time, nine years to the date?

Being told your mother died, your only friend in this world?
You're lonely, sad and grieving, just you and your baby girl?

PRIEST: Oh, my child! Have you ever known mirth?
CHILD: No, Father, just remorse from the day of my birth!

## THE MAN

By: Neldon Neal

Oh! What agony . . . as His arms were jerked
and tied on the post above His head.
"Crucify this man! Crucify this man!"
is what the crowd all said.
With a leering gesture, He flexed His muscles,
so brawny and so strong,
Then the soldier grasped the handle
of the woven bone and glassy thongs.

*Slash* . . .it swept through the air.
It cut deep into His flesh.
The pain and the agony . . .
He could hardly catch His breath.
Time and time again
the whip lashed through the air.
It marred and disfigured
that brave man standing there.

The flesh hung in torn strips.
Why did this man not die from pain?
He was just a Nazarene.
Jesus Christ was His name.
The soldier's arm was weary,
too tired to swing the whip again.
Why should he waste his time?
He thought he'd killed this man.

But no! What did he see?
This man he'd beaten took a breath.
Jesus of Nazareth had surely cheated death.
"Stop! You Fool! You'll kill Him!
Cut Him down from the stake.
Take that bucket of water,
Now, throw it in His face."

The man fell to His knees.
On the ground was flesh and blood.
*S-l-o-w-l-y*, very slowly, onto His feet He stood.
The beating was only the beginning.
A cross, He was to bear.
Soldiers placed it on His shoulders.
While trembling, He stood there.

They led Him onto the street.
He slowly dragged His cross.
In weakness, He dropped to His knees
from the blood that He had lost.
The soldiers grabbed a man named Simon.
He was not a Jew.
Made him carry the cross for Jesus,
lest he'd be beaten too.

Through the mob he carried it,
on up Calvary's hill.
For the man beaten so badly,
He swallowed the bitter pill.
The cross was laid upon the ground
between two thieves that day,
as the figure of a beaten man
slowly lurched their way.

They flung Him to the ground,
the cross beneath His back so torn.
*Whack* . . .the nail went through His feet
and now they raised His arms.
Oh, what pain He suffered
as the nail went through His hand.
The crowd and soldiers jeered and laughed
for He was just a man.

Up . . .Up . . .with that cross,
into the ground with that beam.
As it jarred on the bottom of the hole,
from the crucified came no scream.
Oh, what anguish and torment!
Besides this, a crown of thorns on His head
that pierced His brow and tore His flesh.
From these grave wounds, He bled.

This brave man they crucified
that was nailed on Calvary's tree,
truly was the Son of God,
and willingly died for you and me.
He was taken down from the cross,
then spent three days in paradise.
Then on the third day led captivity free

Yes, Jesus paid our price.
He was resurrected!
He conquered Hell, death, and the grave.
We now celebrate Easter
because of Jesus, who from death was raised.

## RUNNING BACK TO YOU

By: Andre Barfield

O Lord, it's true. I've wandered far from what I know is right.
But now I want to come back home and stay within the light.

I've walked along lonely roads and found no peace within.
And carried troubles, heavy loads that sunk me deep in sin.

Now heaven's light shines through from high, revealing what, and why am I.
Lost, bound, and set apart because I chose to leave my God.

Forgive me, Lord. Renew my heart and make it white as snow.
And when it's done, Andre, your son, shall follow You wherever You go.

**CONQUEROR**
By: Neldon Neal

One day I met a man on life's highway.
He was walking the same way as me.
He told me a sad but true story
about a man who died on a tree.

On a rough old tree He was hung
with spikes through His feet and His hands.
The blood drained from His body
and ran down the cross to the sand.

There were thorns woven together for a crown.
They were jammed on His head.
A spear was pierced into His side.
From these grave wounds, He bled.

His body so beaten and bruised,
taken down when He breathed His last breath.
Wrapped, then placed in a borrowed tomb.
A great man, even in death.

Three days and three nights in a grave,
His soul had gone into Hell.
He walked among souls that were prisoners
where Satan and his demons all dwelled.

Satan surely must have been delighted
to have captured the soul of this man,
with scars on His feet and His side
and the scars of spikes in His hands.

Two days had gone and passed by,
but the third day then came around.
Satan was having a field day
when suddenly there came a sound.

The man who was beaten so badly,
wearing a crown, was walking his way.
He walked right up to Satan
and all of Hell heard Him say:

"Old Devil, give me those keys.
I'm taking your captives with me.
I paid the price for their freedom
when I was slain on Calvary's tree."

Old Satan handed the keys over.
Inside, he was fuming and mad.
While all the demons in Hell trembled,
the captives shouting, rejoicing and glad.

The promise of the great MESSIAH,
their forefathers had told them about
had conquered Hell, death, and the grave.
And now Jesus was taking them out.

A mighty host of Heaven's great angels
were there to escort them home,
where they would live in the presence of JESUS,
their King who sat on His throne.

**GAME OF LIFE**
By: Greg Shelton

Life is a game of chance,
with each step you must take caution,
making the right decisions,
going through life with eyes wide open.

Of course! You'll make mistakes along the way,
from each one you must learn a lesson.
For if you don't you'll soon find,
failure can become an obsession.

You must look to God for that knowledge
that quenches your every thirst.
Stop looking to man for the answers.
It was he who put problems here first.

Once you have done this,
leave your fate in His hands,
'cause if you have faith and good health,
you'll find you're truly a blessed man.

## WHY ME?

By: Robert 2X Williams

I heard the walls laugh at me as the pain and pressure overtakes me.
Crouched in a fetal position, trying to escape reality,
I can't breathe 'cause there's no air in my cell.
I can't see 'cause there's no light here in Hell.
Many days I lay blinded, confined a prisoner of this plantation.
I feel the walls are closing in; I've got this suffocating sensation.
"Why me?" I ask as my thoughts drift away.
"Why me?" I ask, "Do I have the strength to endure another day?"
Many moons I've walked and fought in the valley of the shadow of death,
wondering what is my mission and when I'll take my last breath.
If it weren't for bad times, I wouldn't have any.
Enemies, foes and rivals? Yeah, I've got plenty,
along with attitudes and affiliations,
restrictions and limitations
trials and tribulations,
temptations and negative motivations.
I stay in a hell of a situation.
Why me?
Was it something I was suppose to see, but couldn't see,
due to my mental blindness or my grim perception of reality?
Did I miss my calling or take for granted the gift you gave me?
Or was it the brother I killed in the street, whose life I took unmercifully?
You knew I wasn't perfect, a weak sheep with no shepherd to guide me,
born in sin-bred iniquity,
a grim reflection of this society.
Why didn't you intervene?
For you knew the path I'd be taking.
Why did my father's seed live?
Why didn't I die when my mother's water was breaking?
"Why me?" I ask. I feel the last breath within my soul.
"Why me?" I ask. I lose consciousness and my hands turn cold.
"Why me?" I ask. I see light in the darkness and hear a voice from behind.
Allah spoke and said; "I chose to purify you with fire.
I did it all because you're mine."

## A TRUE FRIEND

By: Keith A. Sherman

I've never walked on water. I've never turned water into wine.
But I know the One who did. He's the greatest friend of mine.

He brings me joy and happiness and fills my heart with love.
This friend that I am talking about is only found above.

No matter how bad off I am or how awful I may feel,
I just ask Him to help me, and all of my needs He does fulfill.

He said He'll never forsake me or leave me all alone.
He'll stand right at my side 'til the day He takes me home.

This home is like no other, and eyes it never will see.
He said that He is building it to show His love for me.

There will be lots of people there, because my friend is well known.
His name is called "Jesus" and His father sits on the throne.

Now you know why I'm so happy, while many around me are sad and blue.
It's because of my friend, Jesus. He can be your friend, too.

Just ask Him to come into your heart and leave this world behind.
Walk with Him hand in hand, a better friend you'll never find.

He'll give you peace and joy and the happiness you've been searching for.
You'll be with all of us in Heaven to live with Jesus forever more.

## LET ME KNOW

By: Sheldon Gatewood

How can I hold what I can't grasp?
See what I can't envision?
Or own what is not rightfully mine?

I can't touch the sun
yet, I can feel its rays.
Neither can I behold air with my eyes.
Still, I can feel its cool caress on my body.
Am I wrong for wanting something far beyond me?

No matter how many times I stretch,
I can't seem to touch the floor of heaven,
Is my endeavor in vain?
Let me know . . .

## DARE TO CARE

By: David W. Davis

A warmth has come into my life.
I now shall dare to care.
Before I feared to show my heart.
My feelings, I never bear.
The tree of life within my soul,
was sick for lack of love,
Now I see in other's eyes,
a part of God above.

**LIFE'S LADDER**
By: David W. Davis

No tower of man
forever shall stand
the degrading effects of time.
Only through the heart
by the ladder of life
unto Heaven shall he climb.

## GUARDIAN ANGEL

By: Neldon Neal

Last night I saw an angel.
She motioned with her hand.
Then I heard her speak.
She said she is my friend.

She had been watching me.
She watched me through the night.
She is my guardian angel.
Keeps me safe until the morning light.

The gown that she was wearing
was spun from angel dust.
The halo on her head was gold
and silver that would not rust.

The smile that she was wearing,
it was warm and so sweet.
There were sapphires and diamonds
in the slippers on her feet.

I know I wasn't dreaming.
I really saw these things.
My lovely guardian angel
with a pair of angel wings.

She leaves me every morning
but I know I'm not alone.
She will come again tonight
because she is my very own.

**WELCOMED HOME**
By: David W. Davis

Out of the hollow,
by the whispering brook,
I left behind peace,
when compliance I took.
Just to belong,
I became someone else.
Gaining all I could,
I strived for more wealth.
Believing in fools,
I fell in the ditch.
Now I've crawled out.
In peace, I am rich.

## LORD, I COME TO YOU

By: Frederick D. Howell

Lord, I come to you a humbled soul,
knowing I live only because of you
Lost and alone, now in my later years,
still searching for what I'm supposed to do.
The road I've traveled has been long.
I grow weary and many times I've strayed.
I know my life has a meaning, Lord.
Won't you, please, help me find my way?
I'm tired, Lord; seems the hills are growing steeper.
My body grows weak and worn.
My spirit's frayed from misspent youth.
Lord, give me shelter from this storm.
Shine your light on my path, Lord.
Guide my steps 'til my journey here is through.
Help me find and fulfill the reason you put me here.
Don't let it end before I do.
In you, I put all my trust, Lord,
for only you know what lies ahead of me.
And only by your light shall I ever see,
what my life is meant to be . . .

**UNTITLED**

By: Herman M. Travis

Overwhelming at times, my life has often been,
mostly, by my own hand.
For I never loved myself enough to care about much,
not even the man I had become in life.
A shell of an individual, I vaguely recall, seems to invade
my serene state of consciousness.
I pay that man no mind.
He is no longer a part of the equation that equals me,
an oblivious existence from days of youth long gone.
Now, I overcome that which once overwhelmed me
by understanding the person that I once was.
Over these years I have been blessed.
I am thankful for all that I have, and all the seemingly unnoticeable
things I have acquired:
-A heart that loves unconditionally and feels the pain of those
whose conditions become overwhelming.
-Eyes that see further into a future of brighter things to come,
but not so far as to forget about the here and the now.
-Ears beyond my years that hear words never spoken from lips of another,
when their words are silenced by the chaos that surrounds us all.
-Shoulders ready for anyone that may need to lean upon them.
Strong and unrelenting for any burdens that may ensue,
and able to absorb any tears others may shed upon them.
-And a mind able to sustain me through all the insanity I may encounter.
Yes, I am blessed; even when I haven't realized it . . . I am.

# FAITH

By: Corey Louis Hines

*"Faith is the substance of things hoped for, the evidence of things not seen . . .without faith it is impossible to please him."(Hebrews 11:1,6)*

Faith is the foundation of the Christian walk with God. Without this foundation to walk on, we have nothing to stand or build on. When Jesus spoke to the disciples in Luke 6:47-49, he stated, "whosoever cometh to me and heareth my saying, and doeth them, I will show you to whom he is like: He is like a man which built a house, and digged deep, and laid the foundation on a rock: (that rock being Jesus) and when the flood arose, the stream beat vehemently upon that house, and could not shake it: for it was founded upon a rock. But he that heareth, and doeth not, is like a man that without a foundation built a house upon the earth; against which the stream did beat vehemently, and immediately it fell; and the ruin of that house was great." So you see, faith is the key that determines whether you, the house, can stand against Satan and his devices, the stream. The Bible tells us in Romans 10:17, "faith cometh by hearing, and hearing by the word of God." Bear this important fact in mind.

Now faith is simply belief. If one doesn't believe, there's no way one can receive anything from God. Of all the people that Jesus healed, if they had no faith, He would not have been able to heal them. Faith, to me, is the key that opens the door to God. What we do after we have opened the door determines our success as soldiers for God. If one didn't believe when he accepted God's calling, then his walk, thus far, is in vain. To believe is to have faith, and without faith we cannot please God.

True faith must be based solely on scriptural facts. Unless our faith is established on God's word, it is nothing more than superstition, speculation or presumption. All of these things are impressions, which fail us in a time of need; faith does not. Since true faith is anchored on scriptural facts, we are certainly not to be influenced by impressions. Faith is "evidence of things not seen."

Look at the entire 11th chapter of Hebrews. Every person mentioned in this chapter had faith. They believed in that which they could not see. From this faith all things were added unto them. The same applies to us today. Everyone knows that evidence must be based on facts. We start from this principle when we are born again. Our belief (faith) should stand directly on the eternal fact of the redeeming death and resurrection of our Lord and Savior Christ Jesus as recorded in John 3:16 and 1 Corinthians 15:1-4. This is the faith by which we began and it's the same faith by which we are to STAND (1

Corinthians 10:13) and WALK (2 Corinthians 5:7) and LIVE (Galatians 2:20). "As ye therefore have received Jesus Christ the Lord (by faith) walk ye in Him" (Colossians 2:6).

Faith has to do with the word of God; it has nothing to do with impressions or probabilities. The area of interest of faith begins where probabilities cease, and sight and sense fail. With the natural eye, no one can see or understand faith, only with the spiritual eye and mind. Faith must be based on certainty. There must be definite knowledge of God's purpose and will for the individual. Without that there can be no true faith. For example, it is certain that Jesus died on the cross for our sins. This is a fact that faith needs to rest upon.

Opposition always increases real faith, while false confidence (impressions, probabilities) is damaged and discouraged by it. Those that have real faith know through the opposition that they can endure. Look at the story of Job. There can be no immovable facts that faith rests on. Then it's altogether simpler for us to walk in light of them. From this God can and will build us up in the faith just as he did with Abraham, Moses, Aaron, etc. God delights in increasing the faith of His children. Abraham, Moses and Aaron's faith come to mind. We often reject trials from God, just as they did. Trials and tribulations, difficulties and sometimes, even defeats are the very food of faith.

I was once a very active crack-cocaine user. At times, I felt that there was no help for me, mainly, because I had no faith in God to be able to see my weakness. I didn't trust in Him to deliver me. Concerning my faith, I was in the negative on the scale. I had been in several different treatment facilities for my drug abuse, to no avail. This was my faith being exercised in the wrong thing. Those of us who have been called and chosen from God to do His will, can only be renewed, restored and transformed through His treatment plan. I didn't understand this at the time of my addiction. My life seemed to be one endless trial after another because my faith was in the things of this world. In other words, I was lusting instead of believing. And all who walk according to the lust of this world shall pass away (1 John 15:15-17), meaning spiritually, then physically. There were times when I would wake up in vacant buildings or places that didn't fit the environment that I was accustomed to, and I would say to myself, "I'm not going to get high today," or "I'm all together finished."

Without faith in God, there was no way I could have stopped on my own. I had been called and chosen to serve God. So, until I submitted to the will of God and not that of my own (simply believing God's word), I could not be delivered. Only God can and will deliver those that He's chosen. But He can't until we believe, have faith that He will. When I finally realized that through God and His word that I could be delivered from my trial, if only I had faith in Him, I started believing. From that time on, I've believed. So it was through my trials and oppositions, my faith developed and began to work for me instead of against me. Without trial and opposition in our lives, sometimes there is no room for faith to manifest. And without faith there's no work we can do for God through His Son Jesus Christ. This supports James 2:26.

For enlightenment on faith, read James 2:14-26. Some people will shake their heads at the things that we've gone through, not knowing the reasons why we went through so many oppositions. But, the end result is still the same for all of us, there are those that are opposed severely and those that aren't. It comes together. There are diversities and different administrations for the same purpose.

So build yourself up to God on faith, so that you can stand, and we can see each other in eternity. And remember, ". . . whatsoever is born of God overcometh the world: and this is the victory that overcometh the world . . . but he that believeth that Jesus is the Son of God" (1 John 5:4,5). But if we don't believe, we cannot succeed. All who do believe (have faith) will overcome, and receive numerous blessings according to Revelation 2:7,11,17, 26-28.

## PLEASE SEND ME AN ANGEL

By: Steven J. Anderson

I look to the sky, as it grows in the hills.
I tell the sky just how I feel.
God, if you can hear me, there's something to do.
Please, send me an angel. If you can, send two.
There's a place I'm needed, but here I remain.
I'm needed right now, like the desert needs rain.
My heart is with them, though we can't touch.
Can your angels please tell them, I love them so much?
Will they always be there, right by their sides?
Watch over them, when they go for a ride?
Tuck them in, and give them a kiss?
Tell them, it's them that I miss.
If times are hard, give them a smile.
For when this is over, I'll cover the miles.
To bring me back, to hold them tight.
To be there beside them throughout the night.
God, if you can hear me, there's something to do.
Please, send me an angel. If you can, send two!

## I THIRST

By: WM E. H. Wallace

In the gospel of John 19:28 it says: "After this, Jesus knowing that all things were now accomplished that the scripture might be fulfilled, saith, 'I thirst.'"

Webster's Dictionary defines thirst as:

> *the sensation of need for water; desire to drink; strong desire for anything, as a thirst for learning.*

I thirst! In the same way that the human body needs water to live, so does the spiritual body need spiritual water to live. God is the source and the water is the Word.

I thirst! It's incredible that Christ, the water of life, the one who satisfies the eternal thirst of our souls, cried for water. The blessing of these words become understandable when we realize that Jesus was willing to suffer physical thirst so that our spiritual thirst could be grounded for all eternity.

This truth is taught in John 4:13,14. Jesus, conversing with the woman at the well said, "Whosoever drinketh of this water shall thirst again. But whosoever drinketh the water that I shall give him shall never thirst; but the water that I shall give him shall be in him a well of water springing up into everlasting life."

We forget that God has chosen us for a purpose: to tell the truth that there is but one God. There is a phrase running through the last 5 chapters of the book of Judges: "Every man did that which was right in his own eyes" (Judges 17:6). Today, as back then, we find people falling away from God and worshipping the gods around them. We must stop trying to quench the thirst of our spiritual being with the false gods of liquor, drugs, sex or money.

We can drink the water of life freely. In John 4:24 it says, "God is a spirit: and they that worship Him must worship Him in spirit and in truth." How can you worship God in truth if you don't know the truth? We've got to seek God where he will be found. He and all of his truth are found in the word. "Blessed are they which do hunger and thirst after righteousness: for they shall be filled."

Jesus Christ thirsted, suffered, and died on the cross so that we might have the right to God's greatest gift, eternal life. God gives us his invitation in Revelation 22:17 when he says, "Let him that is athirst come. And whosoever will, let him take the water of life freely."

The greatest that ever lived was only a servant for God. Without that thirst for the truth, which is found in His word, we cannot serve Him or His purpose for us in this life. Our God is a provider and a deliverer. "O taste and see that the Lord is good: blessed is the man that trusteth in him." This is my challenge to each and every one of you.

In closing, II Chronicles 7:14, God tells us, "If my people, which are called by my name, shall humble themselves, and pray, and seek my face, and turn from their wicked ways; then will I hear from heaven, and will forgive their sin, and will heal their land." Only God can quench our spiritual thirst. Jesus Christ and His word are the answer. We can't seek His face if we don't seek His word. Therefore, get thirsty!
Amen.

## ONE MORE DAY, ANOTHER TOMMORROW

By: James K. Harbin

How much longer, my dear Lord,
the pain shall I have to endure?
One more day? Another tomorrow?
When will I know for sure?

All the strength I now have,
is only because of you.
Tell me, my dear Lord,
what is it I need to do?

My faith is ever so strong.
On you, I always depend
for one more day, another tomorrow,
right now and always 'til the end.

For one more day, yet another tomorrow
I'll walk slowly and softly each day.
For I know you'll always be with me,
each and every step of the way.

## AN EYE FOR AN EYE

By: Randall McPheeters

In the dark, dark corridor, the mumbled, non-sensual monologue of Glen Morgan continued as always. Father Kyle walked slowly toward the sound, glancing briefly into the barred cells he passed. He stepped softly trying not to disturb the inmates dozing on their narrow, flat, metallic bunks.

Finally, through the bars, Father Kyle could see the large, oafish looking Glen Morgan. Glen was facing the blank rear wall of his small cell, talking to the wall as though it was a person. Father Kyle cleared his throat to get Glen's attention.

Glen growled when he saw the priest. The slack look on Glen's hulking face contradicted the anger in his burly voice and the tension evident in his immense knuckles, now menacingly white, clutching the bars between the two men.

"What you want?"

"I only want to bring you comfort, my son."

"Then leave!"

Glen turned back toward the rear wall to resume his previous conversation.

"Please, Glen, let me pray with you. I only want to show you the forgiving love of God."

"Is your God the one that says I die, 'eye for eye'? Take Him with you and go!" Glen said without turning back toward the priest.

Father Kyle bowed his head, "I will pray for you, Glen. It is not God who wants you dead, but men."

Glen gave no indication that he heard the priest's last comment. He resumed his mumbled nonsense. Father Kyle began the long, lonely walk back to the gate. On his way, he met Charles Phillips, Glen's defense attorney. They passed each other with a cursory nod and no words.

"Glen, how are you?"

The cheerful tone of the lawyer's voice broke Glen from his monologue. He turned and smiled as he approached the bars to greet Charles.

"I good to go," Glen said with his slack-faced grin. "Can I go home now?"

"No, not yet," Charles chuckled and began leafing through some papers. "I need to talk to you about the little girl."

"I tell you, I don't see no little girl."

"I know, Glen, I want to know if you heard the little girl or anyone else that day…before the police came."

"No, I tell you already. I was sleeping and hear nothing."

"I remember, but the girl's brother said that he saw her going into the woods that day with a guy who looked like you."

"I know Johnny! I seen Johnny lots of times. Him smart." Glen bobbed his huge head.

After an hour of incoherent recollections, Charles left empty-handed. Glen lay on his bunk exhausted.

As he drifted into a half-sleep, Glen thought he saw a glimmer in the upper corner of his cell. It seemed to grow and swim toward him. Frightened, he wanted to scream for the guards, but he was frozen in his bunk and the words would not come.

The glimmer became an immense light, larger than Glen himself. It hovered just beyond the edge of his bunk. The formed, concrete walls of his cell seemed to disappear as light filled the tiny room. Glen tried to look away from it, but it seemed to be everywhere. There was no shape or form in the light, but somehow it reminded Glen of the statute of an angel outside the church near his home.

Little by little the fear dissipated, replaced by curiosity. He wanted to talk to the light or touch it. He tried to ask a question but his voice was just a soft, hoarse croak. He tried to swallow and repeat the question but the light became brighter and a beautiful voice came from within.

"Be at peace, Glen; I mean you no harm."

Glen was shocked that the light knew his name, but a soothing calm swept over him and he asked, "Who are you?"

"I am Gabriel, an angel of the Lord."

Anger and fear replaced Glen's calm. "The Lord want me dead!"

"I told you, Glen, I mean you no harm. Why are you afraid?"

" 'Cause you here to kill me!"

"No, Glen. Who told you the Lord wants you dead?"

"These guys!" He said waving his big hands in all directions as though the answer to the question should be obvious.

"And did they tell you why the Lord would want you dead?"

"The Lord say, 'eye for eye.' I die for the little girl."

"Do you know the Bible, Glen, where the words 'an eye for an eye' are found?"

"Momma used to read the Bible to me, but I'm not too smart."

"That's okay. Do you know who Jesus is?"

"Sure! Everybody knows He's the Lord!"

"That's right, He is the Lord. He doesn't want you dead either. He tried to tell people long ago when He walked with them, but the people failed to understand."

"If God doesn't want me to die, why do these guys want to kill me?" Glen struggled with the idea. Then, suddenly, hope lit his dark eyes. "Why don't Jesus come and tell 'em again so they won't kill me?"

"He has already told them that the law was fulfilled, but the children of Israel failed to believe. They still follow the law."

"That's what they told me, 'It's the law.' The little girl's dead and 'eye for an eye' I gotta die."

"The law these people speak of does not apply to you, Glen."

"So the Lord won't let them kill me?" Glen asked, hopefully.

"No, Glen, I will take you with me, but you must write something for me first."

Glen, filled with relief that his life was no longer in danger was enveloped by the eternal peace this light brought. With a newfound joy, he reached under his bunk and shuffled some things around; then he came up with a marker and a wide grin. "Write on what?"

"Write it on the wall."

As Glen turned to the rear wall of the cell, the light touched his hand. Experiencing love like he had never known, he began to write.

The warden elbowed his way through the crowd of guards and doctors gathered at the door of Glen Morgan's cell.

"He's dead all right," a cold voice said within the cell.

"Get out of the way!" The warden cried as he entered the cell, "How did he die?"

"I haven't a clue," the doctor smiled and looked to the warden with a shrug. "He is in perfect condition except that he's dead."

The warden was momentarily distracted as Father Kyle shouldered his way into the cell. "God in heaven! What is that?" Father Kyle exclaimed in disbelief, staring past the warden at the wall.

The warden turned toward the wall noticing for the first time the message that had been written there. "One thing is for sure, Glen didn't write it. He couldn't read or write."

"Even if he could," Father Kyle said as he made the sign of the cross, "I doubt even Glen's innocence could have communicated such a divine message."

***IF YOU CONTINUE TO JUDGE YOUR BROTHERS BY THE HEBREW LAW, YOU WILL SUFFER THE FATE OF THOSE TO WHOM THE LAW WAS GIVEN.***

As Glen followed the light through the ceiling, he looked back to see the warden mouthing the words he read and shuddering from the chill each word chased up his spine.

**THIS MAN FROM GALILEE**
By: James K. Harbin

There once was a great man.
A story of Him was told to show
the miraculous things He did on earth,
so many years ago.

Several versions I have heard,
but there is only one that's true.
What His purpose was on earth,
it included both me and you.

When He was a young boy,
a carpenter was He.
But as He grew older,
a fisherman of men He came to be.

He traveled from city to city
teaching the works of God,
followed by twelve disciples
with every step He trod.

Miracle upon miracle He performed.
Changed water into wine, made the blind see.
He was called the Messiah,
this man from Galilee.

He was the Son of God, no doubt.
For this He was sentenced to die
by Pilate. The Roman king
delivered this man to be crucified.

A crown of thorns, they made Him wear.
Whelps, He bore as they pierced His side.
They nailed Him to a rugged cross
and left Him there until He died.

He paid the price with His love.
He suffered pain and agony.
With His sacrifice, we might be saved
because of this man, one day on Calvary.

## I AM A PRISONER

By: James K. Harbin

To a prisoner within these walls so gray,
each day often seems the same.
Most of them are filled
with heartaches, loneliness and pain.

Many sleepless nights, I have spent
within this prison cell,
praying for knowledge and hope
to retreat from this man-made Hell.

My eyes have cried a river of tears
for loved ones I hold so dear.
I wish things could have been different
throughout the passing years.

Some people may think they are different,
but that is really not the case.
I wonder how they would act,
if they were in my place.

Now society says that I'm no good.
I think they are too blind to see
The same God that loves them,
also loved and died for me.

## UNITED WE STAND

By: Tammie Yaniro

God's masterpiece surrounds us like a flawless symphony,
from the ocean to the mountains in their brilliant majesty.
In every crystal snowflake, every painted sunset hue,
and the panoramic splendor of a twilight's velvet blue,
every animal and flower, every child's smiling face,
is a tender thing of beauty and individual grace.

Everything in nature serves a purpose for the "whole"
and a common thread connects us,
heart-to-heart and soul-to-soul.
So appreciate diversity in every form and culture
from the Eskimo and Pygmy
to the dolphin and the vulture.
The world's a perfect forum for our creativity,
all the players with their own unique design and destiny.

And it's our responsibility to cherish Mother Earth,
protecting her fine balance and preserving all her worth.
So broaden your horizons.
Share your gifts and take a hand.
Then we can ease the conflicts
that spill poison on this land.
The bottom line is simple but it's easy to lose sight.
We're here to grow and be as one
not prove who's wrong or right.

To face our fears and learn to trust
may be the hardest test.
We won't reach our Nirvana
'til we break down every wall . . .
*United we will rise above; divided, we will fall.*

## WALKING

By: Terry Linster

*"For thou hast delivered my soul from death: wilt not thou deliver my feet from falling, that I may walk before God in the light of the living?" (Psalm 56:13)*

Walking in Christ is what a Christian, a true believer, strives to do. What does a Christian display or what are the characteristics of faithfully walking in Christ? The first thing exhibited in the Christian is the "new life" which is graciously given to all who are His chosen. "Therefore, we are buried with him by baptism unto death; that like as Christ was raised up from the dead by the glory of the Father, even so we also should walk in newness of life." (Romans 6:4)

Let us understand that the "baptism" spoken of is not the immersion in the water or ceremonial baptism but rather the baptism of the Holy Spirit pouring over and into you upon salvation. If you have been saved, you know what I speak of. It's that newness of desire within us, the desire to rid ourselves of that old sin-filled life and to do what is right in the sight of God alone.

The second characteristic of a Christian's walk is faith. "For we walk by faith, not by sight." (2 Corinthians 5:7) This is the faith of our Lord and Savior Jesus Christ by whom we are saved. We grow in faith just as we grow in Christ. How is this done?
"So then faith cometh by hearing, and hearing by the word of God." (Romans 10:17) This is accomplished by hearing God's Holy Word spoken, by reading, studying, meditating, praying and obediently applying His Holy Word to our daily lives. As we learn a new truth, we place it within ourselves and act upon it (put it to work). "Even so faith, if it hath not works, is dead, being alone." (James 2:17)

True faith requires an action, or "works." Works do not bring faith and alone is meaningless to God. Likewise, faith without action or works is also dead in the sight of God for no fruit is yielded for what has been planted. Our walks reflect what He has graciously bestowed upon us. Each good work proclaims Christ as King of our lives and reflects whom we serve. "For whatsoever is born of God overcometh the world: and this is the victory that overcometh the world, even our faith." (1 John 5:4)

The third element is the characteristic of "spirituality" of the believer. "This I say then, walk in the Spirit, and ye shall not fulfill the lust of the flesh." (Galatians 5:16) To be in the spirit is to walk according to God's holy word (the Holy Bible) and not according to what is acceptable by the majority of this world. Today we see many churches accepting or openly tolerating within its walls that which is unacceptable in the sight of God no matter how they wish to interpret His Holy Word.

Some of us have seen the expulsion of prayer from schools along with discipline, respect, and responsibility; the open acceptance of homosexuality even in pulpits; the mating, legitimately, of same sex partners, adoption of children into unholy unions; the countless millions murdered by abortion and now this new unholy craze called partial-birth abortion. The legislatures and courts of our land preach separation of church and state yet in their own hypocrisy have chaplains and prayers in legislative meetings and have people place their hand upon God's Holy Word in the courts to be sworn in "so help me God." It's getting worse each day with our society reflecting this ungodliness.

This is called being in the flesh, having God's Holy Word yet going another direction (to hell). We, who believe, know this battle within each of us, yet the gift of God has nullified its purity over each of us. This I will name and claim joyfully and gladly to Him. "If any man teach otherwise, and consent not to wholesome words, even the words of our Lord, Jesus Christ, and to the doctrine which is according to godliness; he is proud, knowing nothing, but doting about questions and strife's of words, where of cometh envy, strife, railings, evil surmisings, perverse disputing of men of corrupt minds, and destitute of the truth, supposing that gain is godliness: from such withdraw thyself. But godliness with contentment is great gain. For we brought nothing into this world, and it is certain we can carry nothing out. And having food and raiment let us be therewith content." (1Timothy 6:3-8) "Teaching us that, denying ungodliness and worldly lusts, we should live soberly, righteously, and godly, in this present world." (Titus 2:12) "Seeing then that all these things shall be dissolved, what manner of persons ought ye to be in all holy conversation and godliness?" (2 Peter 3:11)

Being in the spirit is placing God first, above all else in this world because everything in and of this world will be gone. So the believer who relies on Him will never perish. This places God first, all else below Him, on our list of "things to do." Do we place Him behind while we try to get ahead? Do we show Him what we can do and if we fail then seek Him or vice versa?

The fourth characteristic is "consistency." "And He said to them all, if any man will come after me, let him deny himself, and take up his cross daily, and follow me." (Luke 9:23) Being a Christian is not something we do on a given day but how we are everyday. It is being consistent. This is growing, for we know that as a child we had to learn. So it is now, as we learn, we apply. As we apply, we walk each day. This is not saying that we are infallible because we surely are not. We make mistakes and get mad, but we also strive for that righteousness of Christ. When we fall, we have a means to get back on track. The Holy Word confirms this: "And it shall be with him, and he shall therein all the days of his life: that he may learn to fear the Lord his God, to keep all the words of this law and these statutes to do them: That his heart be not lifted up above his brethren, and that he turn not aside from the commandment, to the right hand, or to the left: to the end that he may prolong his days in his kingdom, he, and his children, in the midst of Israel." (Deuteronomy 17:19-20) "Till I come, give attendance to reading, to exhortation, to doctrine." (1Timothy 4:13)

We are enabled to live constantly only by knowing and applying the Scriptures as we learn them. How did Christ respond to others? He responded by and from the Scriptures. That, brethren, is our example in the greatest sense. Therefore, we must read, study, meditate, pray and apply the Scriptures daily in our lives. I say daily because each day is a new one and must be reinforced to keep us on the righteous track set before each of us.

The fifth characteristic I need to mention is "love." Not physical attraction but rather that Godly or agape love like God has for His creations (us). "And thou shall love the Lord thy God with all thine heart, and with all thy soul, and with all thy might." (Deuteronomy 6:5) "O love the Lord, all ye his saints, for the Lord preserveth the faithful, and plentifully rewardeth the proud doer." (Psalm 31:23). "And walk in love, as Christ also hath loved us, and hath given himself for us an offering and a sacrifice to God for a sweet smelling savior." (Ephesians 5:2) "And we have known and believed the love that God hath to us. God is love; and he that dwelleth in love dwelleth in God, and God in him." (1 John 4:16)

I don't believe there is much to be added to the above Scriptures. A person who is saved understands this agape love. Take the time to go through the Scriptures on the subject of love and you will be amazed at the number of times it is used.

The sixth characteristic is "caution." "See then that ye walk circumspectly, not as fools, but as wise, redeeming the time, because the days are evil. Wherefore be ye not unwise, but understanding what the will of the Lord is." (Ephesians 5:15-17) "As ye have therefore received Christ Jesus the Lord, so walk ye in him." (Colossians 2:6)

We, as Christians, walk wisely by knowing and applying God's Holy Word to our daily lives, therefore seeing the world for what it truly is and what God has given to each of His children. We learn the will of our Lord through His Holy Word. That is why we daily read and study scripture, to plant and nature His seed within us.

The seventh characteristic of a Christian's walk is "illumination." "But if we walk in the light, as he is in the light, we have fellowship one with another, and the blood of Jesus Christ his son cleanseth us from all sin." (1 John 1:117) This is another characteristic that is really self-explanatory. We have each witnessed someone who has that glow of faithfulness and have probably seen someone speak a kind word when confronted with anger. I know I have witnessed this heavenly glow; some call an aura, when in fellowship or when I spoke with a faithful Christian before I was saved.

The last characteristic is "Christlikeness" which, to me, is all of the others combined. "He that saith he abideth in him ought himself also so to walk, even as he walked." (1 John 13:15) "For I have given you an example, that ye should do as I have done to you." (1 John 13:15) Christ is our example. We know that by following His example and His will we cannot go wrong because we are following in His footsteps. Look at these Scriptures sometime: Matthew 11:29, 16:24, Romans 15:5, 2 Corinthians 10:1, Philippians 2:5, Colossians 3:13, Hebrews 3:1, 12:2, and 1 Peter 2:21.

Within these writing, my brethren, it becomes apparent that the only way to ensure we are walking in Christ is simply by reading, studying, meditating, praying and applying His Holy Word, the Holy Bible, to our very existence daily. As we take in His word we push out the garbage and replace it with the characteristics of Christ. The amount of time we spend in Scripture, in fellowship with the brethren, and in His blessed presence is reflected: spend a little time and little is shown. So it's in our hands and our hearts as to who we serve and who we strive to emulate.

The elements or characteristics given were derived from my Thompson's Reference Bible, which is a tremendous tool for me in studying God's Holy Word.

It is that blessing that aids me in writing many things. The Holy Ghost guides me when doing the research, compiling and writing. If this has been of any benefit to anyone, please take the time to give thanks where it is deserved, to the living God, the precious Son, and the blessed Holy Ghost, by which inspiration is given to each of us. "They shall speak of the glory of thy Kingdom, and talk of thy power." (Psalm 145:11)

May God be with each of you, today and evermore. Amen.

Your brother in Christ,<br>
Terry Linster

# SOCIAL MADNESS

## EDUCATION, COMMUNICATION, LIBERATION

By: Reiko E. Hailes

The effect and significance
of the most High's existence
will be determined by mankind's resistance
of the divine laws
without flaws.
We originated in Alkebelan,
enslaved and forced to build this modern-day Babylon.
The revelations had no influence on the Emancipation Proclamation.
Our past and current situation
shows the dehumanization
through generations
of pain and miseducation
and lack of communication
And yet, we still haven't gotten our liberation.
Study the destruction of African civilizations.
Come to the realization
that we need spiritual rejuvenation
to rear an earthly, heavenly destination,
a product of my environment, my inspiration
went out the windows
as I've lain on my pillows
I've dreamt about the assassination of my heroes,
I visualized their plight,
Could it be? My elders have become soft and gullible,
the youth are no longer controllable.
blurry has become my sight,
I sit dumbfounded wondering if we've given up the fight,
return of the consciousness
awareness
to reveal the intelligence that's hid,
for the men with kids
who have enough time to get drunk and high off of an ounce,
but not enough time to bounce
your kids to school or to the park,
so we end up in the dark,
never really seeing the light,
we end up being like our sorry dads,
this scenario has become a fad and it's sad
to witness this modern type of inbred sickness.

## EXTREME MOTIVATION

By: Anthony Meadows

Gutter water flows blood-red
from one of the young occupants
of these vicious ghetto streets

Hunted, stalked and cut down
by one of the many predators who feeds
on the blood of its inhabitants like vampires

Fear flows through this jungle
like an aromatic, pungent dish
penetrating the walls
paralyzing in its wake

A mother's scream climbs octaves
above the sirens
piercing the hearts and minds
turning fear into rage
and immobility into action

The predators find themselves
surrounded
by enraged black faces
bent towards violence

The screams rise higher
the crowd converges
and out of this is born . . .

**REVOLUTION!**

**THE WAKE UP CALL**
By: Rodney Edward

Let me assure you that I am not prejudice nor am I a black activist. But as an individual and as a people, I want you to know that we are at war. The majority of the people on my side has their eyes wide open but still don't recognize what they are fighting for. I guess that's why I'm writing to try and shed some light on the ill informed:

We've been in the darkness so long
Don't know right from wrong
Ya'll scared to come near it
You ignore the voice in your head, when you hear it

Your enemies are after your spirit
but you think it's all in your mind
But ya'll find out a lot of the reasons
why we are so far behind
is because the system's designed
to keep our third eye blind.

We don't even know who we are,
but the answer ain't far.
Matter-of-fact it's right under, no, above our nose.
But the system we're living in teaches us to keep that book closed.

The reason we have to lie and deceive,
and don't act to get the blessings we are suppose to receive,
is because we act on what we've come to believe.

We are ready to die over a coat
or a necklace around our throat.
Families are sick and tired
of putting their kids six feet deep in dirt
Hear this, but what's worse,
is if it was put in a rap verse,
you'd listen to that bullshit first.

We are losing
what our ancestors' battles were proving.
That's why I am choosing
to reach out so hopefully you will go deep within
and take a good look at the life you're living in

Change is possible, but it starts with you.
All you have to do
is pray to the Father above and ask Him
to forgive you for all your sins
and I guarantee you're sure to win in the end.

**DISENFRANCHISED:**
**What We Do Best**
By: Daniel W. Campbell

Prologue:

What do we do best? Someone recently said it on the radio:
*We covet that which is not ours and call it ambition.*
*We murder the innocent unborn and call it choice.*
*We pollute the air with lies, pornography and heresy and call it freedom of speech.*
*We worship false and belligerent gods and call it multiculturalism.*
*We sell our children to foreign soil and call it pluralism.*
*We promote the point of ineptitude and call it equal opportunity.*
*We submit to blind leadership and call it democracy.*
*We subvert authority and call it justice.*
*We profane individuality and call it universal consciousness.*
*We desecrate the deal and call it science.*
*We abhor our parents and call it freethinking.*
*We rob the poor and call it free enterprise.*
*We lust for blood and violence and perversion and call it entertainment.*
*We seek the private thoughts and affairs of strangers and call it society.*
*And here we remain . . .disenfranchised . . .disoriented . . .disordered . . .*

## DISENFRANCHISED

The United States of America? In God we trust? Give me liberty or give me death? Ask not what your country can do for you? Let freedom ring? Duty, honor, country? United we stand? Tenacity, gumption, discipline? Whereas, we hold these truths to be self-evident?

Divided we fall . . .oneness . . .a lie. A misconception. This is a fruitless faith in the raw concept of equality, justice, fortitude and righteousness. This is the harvest – we have reaped what was sown, and we are left barren in our hearts and minds and souls. We are the godless remnants of a dream gone nightmarish. We embrace violence, homosexuality, greed and divisiveness as inherent normalcy, and we vilify all who seek to uphold moral, ethical, common sense tenets. We embrace total ignorance of the law and we crucify any man of courage who practices honesty and courage and strength. We cast out our children, our elderly, our innocent and we practice all manner of apathy to satisfy our rotted sense of decency. Lies. Nothing new. Nothing is shocking. Nothing is sacred. Sanity is secondary. Self-fulfilling wantonness is the rule, never the exception. We refuse to allow "facts" to interfere with our twisted opinions and beliefs. I am sickened beyond hoping. My personal freedom was long ago taken due to my own misconduct. I have watched my nation fall from greatness to the depths of depravity. Nothing matters now, only the moment. What have we become? Stupefied teenagers are spreading disease and terror. Unfit, disordered parents despise the children they bring into existence. Power-hungry elite crush the weak and deify themselves. Thrown-away infants, godlessness, pornography, evil and lust . . .mind-controlled. No! Not controlled! Content! Agreeable! Unhindered free Americans! This is our choice. These are the results of the subtle tyranny we have incorporated into the fibers of our society.

Blinded by weakness, we embrace pure sin and turn from the light of reason to the darkness of bestial dysfunction. Bereft of pride, we pollute, destroy, ravage and waste. Turning a deaf ear, we ecstatically adopt policies that smack of arrogance, communism, Nazism, terrorism, socialism and Satanism, yet we prey ruthlessly on anyone who dares to uphold a personal belief in faith, race, culture or privacy, and we persecute without mercy the chaste. Every man is a coward. Every woman is a whore. Every natural desire is a foul and unmentionable crime. Love means hate, yes means no, and kindness means only viciousness.

We are pathetic losers, pitiful, wrongly indoctrinated rejects and fools, unheard voices in the roaring silence, broken, beaten, shattered, battered, blasted cast-out bastards of the bloodline of man. I am to blame as is everyone. We are unclean maggots that do not feel compassion or need. We cannot raise our own sick-minded children because the schools have made them into machines of malice. So we want the government to raise them for us. We are too stupid and clumsy to own guns, so we let the government take them from us. We cannot choose our own destiny, so we demand that the government make our destiny. We are too confused and illiterate to choose our leaders by vote, so we ignore our ballots and ignore our incompetence. Yet we raise our voices in unrighteous indignation when our elected officials attempt to gain any measure of sanity in the pursuit of civil reformation. We are too dumb to learn anything if we do find a normal school system, so we drop out and blame all our problems on one another.

We can't control our own emotions so we insist that the government tell us what we need to think and feel. We do not care if the air and water is poison because the government assures us all is safe. The government decides where we can work, what hospital we are allowed to use, and how much of our income is ours. We are too numb to be creative so we let the government tell us what are art, music, theatre and entertainment. We are impotent, so the government provides stimulating drugs and study groups to teach us how to procreate, how to accept immoral treatment, and what feels good. We cannot exist without government assistance, so we choose government-approved partial abortion, allowing murderers to rip fetuses from the womb and stab them in the head with a syringe to suck out the brain. Or we allow unwanted children to be given to unfit families so that another prostitute, porn star, drug addict, or Ritalin patient can plague the world. We want the government to decide our caregivers, and we turn over our most personal thoughts to government officials to correctly declare us a danger to the very society we have created ourselves.

I am statistically dead, cheated of morality, happiness, peace, common decency and respect for human life. My vitality ebbs rapidly and I have no more tears. I am a disenfranchised sufferer responsible for my own demise. I cannot stem the tide of horrifying reality that crushes my soul and extinguishes the last dim ray of hope. I no longer desire that which is unachievable in this cesspool. I have lost all I can lose. I am ashamed to be an American . . . to be human and to be . . .alive.

**THE GOLDEN KEY**
By: Tammie Yaniro

Floating through a dreamscape where my wishes all come true,
where crystals grow like roses and the seas are sapphire blue,
where music softly echoes through the meadows and the trees,
the fragrance of gardenias, blowing gently in the breeze
And I can soar above the peaks of mountains, far and high.
Free, just like an eagle, dodging rainbows in the sky

And everyone's united - there's no envy, greed, or shame.
The fruits are all delicious and the animals are tame.
I wished with all my heart and soul that I could take you with me
back into my waking world, for everyone to see
some of the abundance, joy and peace that are here
And no sooner had I wished it, then a wizard did appear.
Amidst a silvery stardust, pointed hat upon his head,
he patted my arm gently and was smiling as he said,
"I've come to share a message that will launch your noble quest,
the Golden Key to guarantee your dreams will manifest.
For all that you imagine and believe it will come true.
But cease your search for cause; the power lies in you.
With kindness and compassion, look upon your human race.
Lead them, by example, with your courage, warmth and grace
By sharing your uniqueness in your own creative way
You'll change the world a little, for the better, everyday."

I listened very carefully and vowed that when I awoke
I'd practice this philosophy of love for which he spoke.
Now everyday that passes, I have truly come to find,
that everything looks brighter through an open heart and mind.

*A rhyming fable about self-empowerment in the quest for peace on earth and good will toward humanity.*

## MICHIGAN CONVICTS ANTISOCIAL…WHY?

By: Kevin King

The revised Michigan Department of Corrections Mail Policy (PD-05.03.118) has banned sexually explicit pictures, which does include pictures in male publications (a.k.a. freak books). The language in the policy reads as follows:

> *Paragraph EE; "Prisoners are prohibited from receiving mail that is a threat to the security, good order, or discipline of the facility, that may facilitate or encourage criminal activity, or that may interfere with the rehabilitation of the prisoner. The following pose such risks within a correctional facility under all circumstances and therefore shall be rejected" #14. "Photographs depicting actual or simulated sexual acts by one or more persons. This includes photographs included in a publication sent directly from a publisher or a vendor authorized by the facility."*

As a result of past policy revisions concerning prisoner visits and phone use, it has become increasingly more difficult to maintain any existing relationships, and virtually impossible to establish any new relationships while incarcerated. Due to the aforementioned restrictions, prisoners began their own form of social mingling by sitting around a table and secretly showing off their girls in male publications. As piteous as it may seem, it was a prisoner's way of coping in an abnormal environment, men simply trying to have some sort of female interaction.

What 'penological' justification does the department offer for the removal of the only real opposite sex interaction left to prisoners? They use the word rehabilitation. Is it rehabilitative to 'attempt' to create a non-sexual environment? And can a system with a despicable recidivism rate ranging as high as 85% honestly and fairly use such terminology?

Systematically, the department has overzealously restricted every means available in maintaining healthy community relations. Many intuitive individuals believe the implementation of the restrictive policies, not limited to the phone policy, visiting policy and mail policy, have contributed to an obvious increase in homosexual activity in the prison system. One cannot come to the conclusion that such is conducive with good order, discipline, or security in correctional facilities; let alone rehabilitation.

It is evident that we are being driven to become antisocial. If it's true that we become products of our environment, we have to ask what effect all of this will have on our rehabilitative needs? Moreover, how will these restrictive policies better our reintegration back into society?

## GHETTO CHILD

By: Duane Anthony Brown

"The Inner City"…that's what they call my home.
Junkies on the street corner, gang members on the roam

Ghetto Child…

Bag ladies in the dumpsters, winos without cares,
drug dealers workin' out of condemned buildings,
prostitutes rent their wares.

Ghetto Child…

Life here is hard. No time to play or have fun.
Expect the unexpected. Survival depends on your wits . . .
and the size of your gun.

Ghetto Child…

Yesterday was my tenth birthday. Already, I'm a man.
I provide for my Ma and my sisters. This is a cold and dangerous land.

Don't have no education, my teachers are the streets,
something you wouldn't realize if we ever were to meet.

Welfare wants to take me . . .they say I'm runnin' wild.
What they can't seem to realize is, I'm a Ghetto Child.

**IRRESISTIBLE SPELL**
By: Steve York Lent

Fear of God
Where darkness dwells
And lightning strikes
In a blink of an eye
The sky rolls back
And there you are!

Living a perfect
Life of Hell
In an unearthed aftermath!

He'll break ya down!
Kick you around!
How do you know?
You're not dreaming!

It's only an awakening to the
Revelations of pain,
In an irresistible spell!

## THE YOUNG MAN

By: Darryl Payne

Now it was the custom of the people of the Kikuyu tribe, as with most other people of the land mass now known as Africa, that young men and women would go through the various stages of initiation under the various fundis (masters of their arts). While doing so they would be assigned various chores that were beneficial to the tribe as a whole. Thus it was that a young man named Hodari, whose name meant warrior. He was preparing for his job, tending cattle, as they grazed. Hodari was a young man of 10. He was tall for his age. He was as dark as the wood from the heart of the ebony tree (from which polished black carvings are made to this very day). Not long before, he had started his first initiation under the fundi that oversaw the herds of the tribe and was therefore, quite proud of himself in his new status between childhood and adulthood.

"Eat all your food, Hodari," his muma (mother) said as she fed him on this soon to be dangerous and adventurous morning. "You will be out there long this day tending the cattle and you know how you love to eat," his muma gently admonished.

"Yes, dear Muma," he replied. He wondered why his muma still treated him as a little child as she did his little brothers and sisters who had not yet gone through or even started their first initiations. "Kwa heri (good-bye), dear Muma," he said as he anxiously made his way out of the door of the kibanda (hut) and into the fields where the cows were grazing.

Once in the field he got a pleasant surprise. His baba (father), Nguvu, whose name meant strength, awaited him. "Greetings, my mtoto (son)," said his baba.

"Baba!" Hodari cried as he ran to him.

This was indeed an unexpected surprise as his baba and many other men from the village had gone for more than a week in search of a rogue simba (lion) that had killed one or two head of cattle and attacked one of the women by the stream that the villagers used to get water, bathe, and wash clothes. "I have brought you something," his baba said handing him a spear that was at least a head taller than his young 10-year-old frame. "Are you home to stay now?" Hodari asked.

"No, Mtoto," Nguvu said, "I just came to give you this spear."

"But I have not yet gone through the hunting or fighting initiations," Hodari protested.

"I know," said Nguvu, "but the simba is close to our grazing lands and I wanted you to be protected as well as you could be. I must go now and join the others. Do not try to fight the simba should it come, but run to the south by the stream. We think it may strike at our women again since it has had the taste of human blood. Kwa heri," said Nguvu.

"Kwa heri," said Hodari.

Soon Brother Sun was at its peak and Hodari lightly dozed under a baobab tree. After all, Nguvu had said that the men thought it most likely that the simba would attack the unarmed women washing and bathing, not the large horned cattle with a herdsman who now possessed a very large spear. Suddenly, Hodari awoke. The cattle seemed restless. What was that low sound, a growl? Over to the right, Hodari spotted him, a simba larger than any he had seen on his frequent walks with his father. Its teeth were huge and its mouth was red with the dried blood of its latest victims. At first, Hodari froze until he remembered the spear that his baba had brought him just that morning. "Go away, get out of here," he cried, shaking his spear menacingly. The simba only moved closer. Hodari, disobeying his baba, tried to keep the cattle calm while herding them together in the middle of the pasture, all the while screaming at the simba to go away. The simba moved closer as Hodari jabbed at it with his spear, each circled the other trying to find a clear opening to attack. The simba wanted to sink its teeth and claws into human flesh and Hodari wanted to sink his spear deep enough to be fatal and remove this threat to his village. The simba made an unexpected leap knocking Hodari to the ground. Just then, men came from all directions hurling spears into the now still and dying body of the simba.

When Hodari opened his eyes he was back in his kibanda. The drums were beating outside and it sounded as if a huge celebration was going on. He went back to sleep. When he awoke the next day his baba handed him the simba's skin. Nguvu said, "You disobeyed me and did a brave but foolish thing Mtoto. You could have been killed, and where would I be without my eldest son? While others celebrated, your muma and I would have mourned."

"I'm sorry, Baba," Hodari said.

"It's all right, Mtoto," Nguvu said. "You have many more initiations to go through before you are officially a man, but from this day forward I will treat you as the man you have proved yourself to be. Just remember, never again be a foolish man."

Thus it was, the little mtoto, Hodari, grew up to become a mzee (wise man).

*Note: The Kikuyu tribe is an actual tribe found mostly in Kenya. The Kiswahili words used come from the language which Jomo Kenyatta made the official language of Kenya after Kenya gained its independence from England. This language is spoken in the Eastern and Central regions of Africa.

**ARE WE LISTENING?**
By: James C. Johnson Jr.

Do we really listen to people's cries of today?
Are we really listening to people that have something to say?

We may acknowledge someone when their eyes drop a tear;
but some of us won't get involved and turn a deaf ear.

The children need our help. They are out of control.
They are carrying guns to school, committing murder at eight years old!

These tragedies show that our ears are sealed.
How many more have to die? How many more will be killed?

The politicians only listen if it's an election month,
But once the votes are in then they have what they want.

They say Hollywood promotes violence and rap music corrupts our kid's minds,
but to blame it on them, take a number and get in line.

We must address this issue as if we are at war
'cause we're way down in points and it's vital that we score.

The best way to solve this problem is to listen and use our eyes,
Don't be taken by surprise, and stop covering the truth with lies.

As long as we sit back and ignore the warning signs and cries,
society will continue its downward spiral, its genocidal demise.

**PSEUDO-PLEDGE**

By: K. Whiting

It's 7:15 in the morning. The classroom is bustling with rowdy, chatty young adults. A voice over the intercom silences the students. The voice promptly instructs everyone to "please stand for the pledge." The moans and groans from the students begin as they slowly, yet assuredly, stand. As the voice on the intercom begins to recite the pledge, only the teacher and a handful of students join the voice in the pledge, *The Pledge of Allegiance to the Flag of the United States of America.*

Among the many memories of my primary school years, I recall with clarity standing up with pride to say that pledge. I saw it as my duty as a citizen of the United States to say the pledge to the United States. The snickers would come and giggles would follow, still I stood my ground. I recited that oath loud and proud. And why not, I am an American, right? I should show as much love and loyalty to this country as it has shown me, right? Nonetheless, through the years, those questions began to change dramatically. I started to look at this concept of "pledging my allegiance" and taking pride in being an American differently. I found my mind going through a paradigm shift, like the minds of the people discovering that the Ptolemaic system was wrong.

In her book, *Sweet Summer*, Bebe Moore Campbell writes that as early as fifth grade, she began to only "mouth" the words to the Pledge of Allegiance. This action, she states, came after hearing that "Negroes in the south were being beaten by white people because they wanted to integrate lunch counters at drugstores." Secondly, she also saw Black people trying to march and white policemen coming after them with giant German shepherds. All of these events, Campbell writes, brought her to the point of headaches and anger, to the point that she "wanted to punch somebody" while in the middle of saying the Pledge of Allegiance. She points out that her problem was that she did not want to say the pledge. However, she was afraid to not say anything, so she kept opening her mouth, but nothing came out. After that, she says, "I only pretended to say the words. If they were gonna sic dogs on Negroes then I wasn't gonna say some pledge and I wasn't gonna sing 'The Star-Spangled Banner' neither. Not for them, I wasn't."

Today, many people say, "those violent events do not happen to Black people anymore." Still, any person even remotely keeping up with the news can remember the 1998 conviction of two white men in Texas who dragged a Black male behind a truck to his death. In 1999, four white members of the NYPD killed an African immigrant Amadou Diallo on his doorstep with 41 bullets. Plus, in Riverside, California, a Black man was beaten and stabbed by members of the Hammerskin Nation. If one cannot conceive the reality that history often repeats itself, certainly this violence is evidence that it does.

With all these violent acts being committed against Black people in America, am I wrong for wanting to sympathize with Ms. Campbell? Should someone "pledge allegiance" to a country that shows so much hatred and bigotry towards him? These are now the questions that rise in my mind, questions of loyalty to a country that seems to oppress my people rather than allow them to be uplifted and free. It appears that the Jim Crow laws and Black Codes still linger. Malcolm X stated in his autobiography with Alex Haley that, "I have no mercy or compassion in me for a society that will crush people and then penalize them for not being able to stand up under the weight." For a lot of Black people here in the United States, a large sum of that weight comes from trying to be recognized as an American.

For the African descendants residing in North America, there have been many names and titles to categorize them. Among these is the infamous term "nigger," a word that is so psychologically embedded in the minds of the African descendants here in North America that we often refer to ourselves with the same dreadful name. Notwithstanding, there are other insidious labels such as "Colored," "Negro," "Afro-American," "African-American" and "Black-American" that have the same ill-effect, yet are looked upon as the norm. Author, Errol Smith, asked the question, "What should our people be called?" He answers that question with, "Who cares? What's in a name?" He says he believes we are too sensitive on this subject.

On one side, Mr. Smith has a point. Names are just labels that appear on the surface and are only skin-deep. On the other hand, names give a sense of identity. In addition, an inexact label can bring confusion and division amongst a people. This confusion and division is mainly within the body of the African descendants in the United States. Due to the fact that slavery alienated Blacks from their culture and tore down their national and personal self-respect, they are almost left with no identity. Some of us are confused because we do not know what to call ourselves, likewise, we are divided from those who prefer one title to another, for example some would rather be called Black than African-American. The thing is we, African descendants, may never learn our true identity. Our names, history and cultures were torn from us, lost somewhere over the Atlantic. If a descendant of my tribe of 500 years ago approached me speaking in tribal tongue, I would not know what he was talking about. Slavery has left a terrible wound on our identity and cultural pride, which sadly, may never heal.

The bottom line is this, if I am expected to vote as an American, pay taxes as an American and go to war for this country as an American, then I should be looked upon and treated as an American. All those sub-names just bring us further from what this nation's forefathers originally dared to promote: liberty, justice and the pursuit of happiness. My skin is not the darkest achromatic visual value and I am definitely not a 60's and 70's hairstyle. The way the United States speaks of racial equality and a willingness to work with everyone to make a better society conflicts with the actions that promote the Janus-faced society today. Instead of this nation being colorblind, it is blinded by color. Funny though, during the 2000 Olympic summer games in Sydney, no one ever made mention of a Black or White athlete. They were all American athletes. The United States athletes were judged on their ability and skill, not the color of their skin or their ethnic background.

If it takes athletics to bring the United States together, regardless of their color, then maybe we should use it as a medium. Of course, some schools no longer have physical education as a requirement, however, that is another subject. Academic teacher and historian, C. D. Morris, traces the source of our current racial and economic problems to the failure of the United States to deal with the issue during post-Civil War Reconstruction. Moreover, these issues are still not dealt with today. We continue to suffer from a trail of past failures.

With the coming of a new era, perhaps now is the time to make right the past failures. For, if we continue to turn our heads on this situation, it will only worsen. Equality should be seen and felt genuinely amongst everyone, not just spoken of. Or, if we are not ready to right past failures, we could always do something simpler, like, reword the Pledge of Allegiance.

## GHETTO MADNESS

By: James C. Johnson Jr.

Gunshots ring out and disturb a peaceful day,
and a child falls victim from a bullet gone astray.
Drug deals, marijuana and loud music fill the air.
The ghetto's in self-destruct mode and no one really cares.
Houses covered in security bars,
old people scared to turn out the lights.
because drug fiends and murderers
lurk in the darkness of the night.
There's a war on the streets.
People are dying on the frontlines.
Innocent blood is being spilled.
The ghetto glorifies these crimes.
Our children's eyes are eager
to embrace this ghetto madness.
And to see a child die from this life,
just increases my tears of ghetto sadness.

## THE OLD MAN

By: Edward Armstrong

Everyday at twelve o'clock the old man comes,
slowly dragging his feet, for many-a-mile he's done.
Day-by-day he sits on a bench and watches the birds fly by.
Loyal to time and exhausted by men,
I watch the tears he cries.
The lines in his face run long and deep,
his skin darkened by the sun.
People walk by him, ignoring his pain,
for no one has time for a bum.
Yet, there is something special about this man
for his knowledge and wisdom are vast.
But people plan so much for the future,
they have no time for the past.
Forgotten by many and loved by few,
it would seem his life was done.
Yet, despite his hardship, still,
he musters the strength to go on.
I admire greatly that he never gave up on life.
So now and then when I see him, I give him what I can.
For though he is less fortunate than I,
this old man is still . . . a man.

## DON'T MEAN TO BOTHER YOU

By: Edward Armstrong

I yell, "Hey, mister. Do you have a dollar I can have?"
as he crosses the street to avoid my path.
Walking the streets day and night, searching for food to eat,
people close their eyes to avoid seeing what I see.
My clothes are old and torn,
my shoes worn down to my feet.
I don't live in a large house,
for my home has become the street.
I have no friends, only acquaintances in the dark.
As I make my bed, a bench in a park,
people walk by and yell, "HEY YOU! GET A JOB!"
Their opinion of me is that I'm a poor, miserable slob.
They would rather mock me than help me,
leaving me to die in the dirt.
I have become cumbersome to this heartless planet, Earth.
Yet, I remain faithful that one day I'll have a chance,
for even Cinderella had her one enchanted dance.
One day I shall be counted amongst the elite few.
But why should you care about my dreams?
"Sorry, I don't mean to bother you."

## THE COMING OF A GANG-BANGER . . .

By: Kenneth Drake

Born into a very cold and unfair world without any brothers or sisters, he wanted to be a part of something. He longed to be loved. Accepted by very few, he searched for something worthwhile. He cried out for attention from wherever he could find it. Obviously, his parents did not show him any at all. He was often left alone to do as he pleased.

He was a good kid, caught up in a heartless world. With lots of free time on his hands, he decided to hang out with the neighborhood gang. Seeing a certain amount of love between them, he decided to join. Not knowing that they are just as lost and yearning for acceptance. They all were good kids, once. All they ever wanted was to love and to be loved. Now, they'd found it, not at home, but in the bewildered and dangerous streets, accepted, encouraged, bonded, and most of all, loved in these dilapidated streets. That's where he found love, or so he thought.

He now has a family, lots of brothers and sisters. His life will never be the same. The school courses of life have just begun. After joining, he must prove his worthiness and take oaths to keep for life, with life. He must promise to never betray his brother or sister and always be willing to die for his colors. Mayhem commences as he starts stealing cars and shoplifting, along with other misconstrued petty crimes. He is introduced to drugs and alcohol at a very young age. And if he is lucky, he might become an addict instead of a drug dealer, an alcoholic instead of a pimp, or a con man instead of a dead man. But there is a reason behind this madness. He is not doing this for attention anymore. He is doing it for the love of his gang.

Most gang-bangers do not have any idea what a normal life is all about. Most drop out or are kicked out of school. That's sad. But what's worst, they give up on their dreams.

Deep down inside they are only frightened children, misguided, unloved, and all alone. They are not just found in homes of single parents, but in homes that lack love. So take this advice wisely: your child's choices may be limited. They'll end up in one of two places: jail or hell. But it's not too late to help them turn their lives around. Take time out for them, listen to them, and maybe they won't end up in a gang. Their futures are in our hands.

## MR. RAKEEM'S NEIGHBORHOOD

By: Clint Cooper

It's a dark day in the neighborhood.
Pimps pimpin' and whores whorin'
Gunfights and killings, guns a roarin'
Inner city violence, just another day
in the ghetto, it all happens that way.
Just another day in the neighborhood . . .

Crack-mother in the food-stamp line
Jobless daddies buyin' wine
Shootin' galleries, every other house
Thugs, junkies and a louse
Just another day in the neighborhood . . .

Hungry babies with nothing to eat
Crack-head mama just got beat.
Young girl's raped, old women violated.
Deep within me, oh, how I hate it.
Gimme, lend me, can you spare a dime?
That's how some spend most of their time.
Just another day in the neighborhood . . .

With a tear-stained pillow and weepin' eyes,
Through the window I looked.
Just seen another young mother get hooked.
When will this madness stop?
Why are all these dope-dealers on my block?
Where has love and compassion went?
My brothers and sisters lying in the alley bent.
Just another day in the neighborhood . . .

Robbin', stealin', killin', drug-dealin'
Hearts turned cold with no feelin'
Liquor storeowners, lounges and bars
Just another drug dealer with longer cars
Bar fights, gang fights, gunfights, whore fights
That's the activity in my neighborhood all night.
Just another day in the neighborhood . . .

Front porch hoo-chee mamas, with babies in hand
Turnin' tricks up under a fan
With babies cryin' who haven't eatin'
A trick wants his money back, gave her a beatin'
Dead-beat daddies too high to care or want to know
Just lookin' for a hit and another ho.
Just another day in the neighborhood . . .

My mind is furious with rage.
Thinkin' about my neighborhood in this cage.
When will I be free?
I have plans to change my neighborhood, you see.
Do I put a gun back in my hand?
No! I got to change my plan.

Do I come back as a preacher?
Or, could I be a teacher?
If I seek a political position,
Will my voice be recognized among my peers?
Or will it fall upon deaf ears?
My vision's not yet complete.
I hope to have them ready before I hit the streets.
Just another day in the neighborhood . . .

## SWINE HEART

By: Donald E. Tennyson

Sam sensed that something was wrong right away. The air just didn't feel right, it gave him an almost overwhelming urge to flee. His instinct, however, told him to stay put, to keep low and quiet.

Though the room was dark, Sam could make out the interior of his home. It was quiet, unnaturally so. He raised his head just far enough above the sofa so his eyes could scan the living room. He did a slow sweep from left to right, taking in every detail, every sound, every sight, every feel, even every taste.

Suddenly, there was movement off to the left. The air around Sam was instantly electric and foul with the scent of strangeness. Sam's fear turned to panic. The thought of a stranger in the house was terrifying. He lowered his head so fast, he was sure that the intruder had heard him, but no one came for him. He was safe for the moment.

He was alone and he knew it, no one to rely on but himself. Jill and the children had left only a short time ago and wouldn't be back for hours. Hopefully, he could hide until then.

Sam began to think of Jill, little Maggie and Joey. Oh, how much fun he has with them, Jill's soft hands and soothing voice, Maggie's endless attention and precociousness, Joey's rambunctious play that never seems to end. He wished they were here right now. Oh, how he missed them.

He was suddenly struck by a new, horrible thought. What if his family came home while this stranger was still here? What would happen to them? He had to do something, even though every ounce of sense he had told him to stay put, stay quiet, and stay alive. His family trusted him. They depended on him. He couldn't let them down. He had to protect them.

A strange feeling came over Sam, one he had never felt before. He was jolted by a powerful urge to defend what was his. He knew what had to be done. He slowly moved around the sofa to the side that faced away from where he had seen the stranger. He looked around . . .nothing. Maybe the intruder was gone, but before he could imagine that good fortune, he heard movement upstairs. The stranger was upstairs! Probably making himself at home in his bed. Sam became furious at that thought. This interloper had to go, and go now!

Sam ran to the foot of the stairs, bent on tearing this freeloader to pieces. The thought of someone moving into his home uninvited made him sick. He had the urge to urinate right there on the floor. That would show this trespasser who was boss around here. He fought that urge. There were more important things to do at the moment.

Sam slowly climbed the stairs and with every step a new thought occurred to him, What if this intruder was not just looking for a new home? What if he didn't simply want to drive the occupants out, but maybe something worse? Sam pushed that thought out of his mind. He had Jill and the children to think about. He had to protect them, even if it cost him his life.

He got to the top of the stairs and noticed light coming from Joey's room. He cautiously moved toward the room. His senses told him that it was the intruder. Strangely, Sam had no fear, just burning desire to protect. He reached Joey's room and peered in. There he was. The stranger was big! He had shiny skin that covered his whole body, not the colorful skin that his family had. He had a bag that was the same color as his skin and he smelled awful! He was kneeling down beside Joey's bed doing something with his hands. He hadn't notice Sam yet. Sam took this moment of surprise to act. He ran, threw himself at the stranger, knocking him over. Before the intruder knew what was happening, Sam was on him. Suddenly, the room was a lot smaller than Sam remembered. He was bouncing off of tables, knocking over chairs. Toys were flying every which way and this stranger was strong, real strong! He was also fighting for his life, which made him dangerous. He kicked Sam off and before he could react the stranger slammed something hard to the side of Sam's head. The room started to spin. He couldn't allow himself to stop. Something told him he had to stay on his feet or he wouldn't survive this.

Sam shook his head to clear the cobwebs and charged his adversary, dodged a ferocious kick, catching his opponent about mid-thigh, knocking him off balance. Sam took this momentary victory to issue a loud battle cry. He was feeding on his feeling of kill or be killed and he liked it! If only Jill could see him now, she would be so proud and glad she let him into her life.

The intruder regained his balance, turned, stood and fixed Sam with a look somewhere between fear and amazement. No matter, Sam knew he was being challenged. He also knew this would be it, someone was going to leave this house and it wasn't going to be him. Victory always favored the one in possession, well, most of the time anyway.

Sam rushed the intruder, who raised his hand in what looked like a defensive move, but there was a blinding light, a searing pain in his left shoulder and a defining bang. Sam went down, knocked off his feet by some unseen force. He couldn't move.

The intruder walked over and stood over Sam. There was that strange look again. This stranger had the look of utter confusion and disbelief in his eyes. Could he not understand that he would be opposed, or was it that he thought opposition would be more substantial? Sam wanted so badly to fight, but his body just wouldn't respond. He was letting his family down. They would have to find another place to live and it would be his fault. That was the way of things he knew, survival of the fittest; and he obviously was not fit to protect himself, let alone his home.

The stranger turned slowly and with a slight limp, headed out of the door. Sam lay there, thinking how badly he had been defeated, wondering what would happen now. He looked across the room and saw Joey's chair lying on its side. He had never seen that chair, how strange it looked. The whole room was different and it was his fault. He couldn't let this happen. He had to do something. He was still alive and as long as he had breath he had to fight.

Looking at all the destruction in Joey's room made Sam mad and he drew strength from it. Slowly got to his feet. Every muscle in his body hurt and any weight on his injured shoulder was almost unbearable.

He made his way to the door and peered out. The intruder was standing at the top of the stairs about to descend. Sam knew this would be his final chance, his last act in this life. He begged his tired, aching body for just one more fight, just one more charge.

He moved toward the stranger, picking up speed as he went. He had to reach the intruder before he turned around. He was about halfway when his sore shoulder went weak and he stumbled. The intruder turned and raised his hand. Sam knew he wouldn't make it. He leaped toward the stranger with everything he had left.

Everything seemed to happen at once: the bright flash, the loud bang, the feeling of tumbling end over down the stairs and finally, that loud bone-snapping crack, then darkness.

Sam opened his eyes to a bright world, a world of color: purple, yellow, green, and red, the sweet smells of honey and fruit and the sound of children playing. He tried to move and found the pain unbearable. Suddenly, a soft hand was on his head and a soothing voice was comforting him. It was Jill! He realized he was in his bed. He was in his home. He was alive! The children were playing, Joey and Maggie. He had won. He had saved his family and their home. He was the fittest after all.

Sam knew he was hurt and hurt badly, but he would heal. He knew it, just like he knew his family loved him and he loved them, from the tip of his flat nose to the end of his curly, little tail.

## IMMORTALITY ANYONE

By: Ronald Hutton

Immortality seemed to me, the wisest pursuit
of my earthly existence . . .
Immortality . . .
Tell me, what would you do to live forever?
Attaining it soon became the central focus of my life.
What seemed to be the greatest of achievements,
the greatest of gifts, once attained . . .
and oh yes, it was attained,
soon became not a gift, as I had thought,
but rather a curse . . . a nightmare.
Achievement? . . . No!
Punishment? . . . Beyond compare!
Tell me, what price would you pay to live forever?
I am indeed not one to give your kind advice . . .
and surely not one to take advice from,
but I will say this "my friend,"
the price is very costly.
It is something I cannot live with, but I now *must* live with.
I sleep . . .very little.
I hunger . . .always.
I prey . . .on the weak. I MUST!
The lifeless husks of the numberless elderly,
young children and infants I've left scattered over the globe is . . .
an ABOMINATION.
*I* . . .AM AN ABOMINATION.
Forgive me, Father, for I must sin.
I am forced to stand by "helplessly" and
watch my loved ones grow old, whither and die . . .
and yet . . .I change not.
Everything, everyone I love dies, sooner or later,
and leaves me once again "alone" in this wretched,
God- forbidden state of half-life.

I feel for myself both sympathy . . .and disgust!
I pray for death, but it only eludes me!
I'd take my life, but it's much too late.
I've not beheld the beauty of a sunrise, a sunset
or the very sun itself for longer than I care to remember.
Enshrouded by "eternal darkness," I am alone, hungry
And . . ."damned."
The very doors of Hell are opened wide for me.

As I sit in my Eternal Night, I wonder . . .
When all of humanity ceases to exist,
will I still remain alone? Hungry?
Tell me once more,
What would you do to live forever?
I must go now . . .
It's dark and . . .
I'm hungry.

**DON'T BLAME THE CHILDREN**
By: Curtis L. Jones

We read in the paper and hear on the air
of killings and stealing and crime everywhere.

We sigh and say as we notice the trend,
"This young generation, where will it all end?"

But can we be sure it's their fault alone,
Isn't part of it, maybe, our own?

Are we less guilty, who place in their way,
too many things that lead them astray?

Too much money to spend,
Too many books not fit to be read,
Too much idle time and
Too much evil in what they hear said.

Too many children encouraged to roam,
by too many parents who don't stay at home.

Kids don't make the movies; they don't write the books.
They paint pictures of gangsters and crooks.

They don't make the liquor. They don't run the bars.
They don't make the law and don't buy the cars.

They don't peddle drugs that destroy the brain.
That's done by older folks for selfish gain.

Delinquent teenagers! Oh, how we condemn
the sins of the nation and blame it on them.

By the law of the blameless the Savior make known,
who is amongst us to cast the first stone?

For in so many cases ---it's sad, but it's true,
the title "delinquent" fits older folks, too.

## PRISON DAWN

By: Gregory A. Ott

At times sleep is very deep; a dreamless nothingness where all vanishes and time trudges on. Thought ceases and with that I drift away from the mundane visceral imposition of reality, a temporary reprieve, only to have dawn nudge sleep's demise into history as the omnipresent awe, the awe that overlays each day, slowly unfolding its whimsical beauty.

How fortunate are those who reside in the dominion of a rational God, an all-too-human God, restrained by His own morality, unable to giggle at us with tricks of madness - pretty revenge. Others are not so fortunate. In absolute terror I scream, "Hail Absurdity," knowing that absurdity will mock even this, its own praise. What praise can really emanate from the foolish? What God could be occupied by such desire or placated by such meagerness? We pray to fill the void of action's absence. We fear the taste.

Thus, dawn begins. Truth, with its questionable needs, defines perception. Transparent grids of axiomatic logic blanket the day in futile attempts to harness chaos' opera, its grand ole opera. But wait! Did we not manufacture the transparencies, the flippant thing, nest of our verbiage baggage and the moralities? Are they anything more than our devices, our own vices? Yet to gaze into the caldron of chaos, nakedly, arrogantly, to splash, to frolic in the acidic waters is the boldness of the insane. Surely, that is, if done without reason. HA! Have we forgotten that reason is our own desire?

I ask, who but the mad would opt for a broken crutch? Still, I am drawn toward the dawn, compelled to behold the raw sun 'til it scorches the iris and beyond. My arrogance humbled, or perhaps scorned.

Must this be madness or might there be a truth, an infinite truth that defines . . . no thing? I am plagued by a persistent anarchy of thought. Decadence! It is not style. Heaven forbid the pompous to perceive it as such. It is a necessity. The pyre-poignant truth is far too intense to allow for more than a glimpse, more would certainly condemn. Why I am so tortured with awareness? I've done this to myself. I could have been a cat. What has compelled me?

Impassioned arrogance. Might this be possible, dictum for salvage, for peace, for transcendence? Or is this just another action, another enervation? Action is an enervation. However, pure intense action, being for its own sake, perhaps this is capable of mitigating the no-thing-ness of the slayer of reason. Perhaps this will allow truth to be glimpsed once again. Frenzied, we must try, else existence be negated with the brittle fever of the deepest passion. Grip the moment, the now. Complete actualization must be gripped. Any lesser movement, any acquiescence towards restraint, would drain the vitality itself, muddying the symphony with confusion. Frenzied engagement, the complete frenzy that excludes all else, all except the moment itself, for itself, blends with the chaos, creating a pristine orchestration that soothes the caustic cacophony of the Awe; the omnipresent fatality of happiness and its whimsical beauty. Pure action does not expect. It does not emanate from things and calculations. Not bound by desire, it simply is the archetype of chaos.

This must be madness, whirlpools of deed born without temporal purpose unrestrained by desire, without the delimitation of expectations. No! This is not madness, rather the essence of the whim, the whim that giggles at reason and ludicrous delusions. How can Being be praised? How can Being even be, other than by complete maximum commitment? To engage in part is the embrace of fear, an embrace that can only cause one to cower in the mien of the destined end and thus shun what is. Obviate Being!

Desire denies by its very virtue, a virtue that is other than now. Desire is the prison of the Absurd. It is tomorrow, born from the trepidation, the cesspool of fears, that haunt now. It is the enervating quality of the action; the action that negates life for it is less than the pure action of the nebula of Chaos.

Already this has become protracted. In a foolish attempt to thwart the intrinsic decadence, I vomited these words onto paper, draining the passion. It is forced. Passion is one, mocking the chaos with arrogant laughter. I scream at the new dawn with stilled fear. A stalker of moths, a slayer of butterflies, perhaps, but I tremble amidst the possibilities of freedom knowing that it is I who must bear the responsibilities.

Hail Absurdity.

# LOVE

## YOUR LOVE

By: Nathaniel Hamilton

As I lay quietly awake,
listening to the rhythmic beating of your heart,
I feel your beautiful soft skin caressing me like a warm, summer breeze.
Touching me,
rubbing me,
deep soft skin hugging me
like thick blankets of snow in an open forest.

So thick and smooth,
your body making me feel like a complete man.
Squeezing me,
soft lips teasing me,
arresting me,
undressing my will to leave.
And still your love is strong,
for with a love like yours,
I don't mind being wrong.

How can I ever resist the sweet and tender love you give?
For as long as we're together, I'll follow
wherever you choose to live.
Your love blinds me and I can only see your face.
So within your hands I put my heart
to revive this empty space.
I hope you never leave me lonely
as I turn my back and sleep,
because without your body beside me,
my heart would surely weep.

## LIQUID DREAM

By: Donald E. Tennyson

I feel her closeness, her body close to mine.
We became one.
She does not speak
yet . . .
I understand her.
I cannot see her face
yet . . .
she is with me.
We dance the primitive dance of love,
the one that began our existence
I know that this is her game.
She opens and allows me to enter
yet . . .
this is not a new place
even though I've never been here before.
She moves with me.
She knows my actions before I do.
She brings them to me with such force
that I cannot control myself.
This cannot be real for no one knows these places.
No one knows my dark desire
yet . . .
she exposes me.
She challenges me to go higher.
She knows my weaknesses.
I shamefully submit to my humiliation.
I explode in ecstasy and she is gone
No trace of her is left,
only the evidence of our dance
and the memory of the game.

**BETRAYER OF A REAL MAN'S LOVE . . .**

By: Bernard Dabney

You and I started out as loving and caring special friends,
but we became lovers in the end.
You made me believe you really did care,
but now that I need you, you're not there.
You built me up and helped me stay strong,
but now you've left me all alone.
With life, you helped me cope,
by giving me brand new hope.
You told me my love would never be denied,
but when you spoke those words you knew you had lied.

Just as the rainbow follows every rain,
into our lives must fall some pain.
Many miles are keeping us apart,
and now you're breaking my heart.
As the sun begins to shine,
thoughts of you are on my mind.
While the stars are sparkling at night,
I still dream about holding you in my arms tight.
I love you more today,
than I did yesterday.
But that's okay; I'll take the bitter with the sweet.
And oh, how it hurts to accept this defeat.
To you, goes all the fortune and fame,
because on me you ran the lover's game.
So from this day forth, you will be thought of
as a betrayer of a real man's love.

## THE UNDENIABLE TRUTH OF MY THOUGHTS

By: Reiko E. Hailes

How your parents had such a beautiful daughter is a mystery.
And you, physically, are such a sophisticated part of creativity,
that it confuses scientist and evolutionist when they study.
Having you in my life uplifts my spiritual peripheral visuals.
I meditate upon you solely as if you were the only other existing individual.
When we communicate it's like pyramids form into a duplex,
more complex than a skyscraper drawn from an architect's blueprint apex.
To think badly of you would provoke a lifetime of migraine headaches,
more frustrating than measuring the circumference of the earth
after a million earthquakes.

## WEDDING VERSES

By: J. A. Banks (Nantambu)

Love chose me the very day that I realized you.
Things changed.
Rising had a purpose,
which was as hypnotizing
as waves crashing.

While beating ever so gently against the shores of my heart,
desire required me to open it to you
and we become as one.

I am revealing what lies deep within my soul
a union,
undeniable to behold.

As the sun illuminates the moon
so shall it be . . .
You and I, together
You and I, forever

**ODE TO DOUBLE "D"**
By: Sharon White

Oh, glorious material creature,
pillar of perfection,
how I adore you!
You engulf me in your softness,
spoil me with your comfort.
You give me control.
With your willingness and support
I maintain a certain confidence in my stride.
You are indeed a friend.
One I can depend on to uplift me.
When I come for you
you are there
ready,
to be received with open arms.
Yes, there are others,
but none as satisfying as you.
My keeper of secrets:
    My strength!
        My Wonderbra!

## MOONLIGHT KISSING

By: James Butler

Yesternight we kissed under the moon
Its beams surrounded you and me.
We embraced in its enchanting illumination
sharing tenderness for God to see.

We stood aglow like bright holy angels.
Fast heartbeats felt, chest pressed to chest,
succulent kisses soft and warm,
moonbeams exposing sweet cleavage of soft breasts.

Romantic beneath a full moon
as one, intertwined,
mine all mine and thine all thine.
Kisses heady as choice old vintage wine.

Oblivious of the world, veiled by night,
we seemed to inhabit the earth alone,
I, man, you, woman,
We, flesh and bone.

Passion fervent and sealed by silvery beams,
love waltzed under the moon through our kisses.

## AIROTCIV

By: Carlton J. Johnson

Images of you,
to the mind are sweet.
Dreaming of the first,
and next time we meet.
I compare you to,
a single red rose,
a cool waterfall,
or the river from which it flows.
But the beauty you possess,
there is nothing to compare,
for you're unique and special,
a person so rare.
Your attractiveness is
not merely skin deep.
Your inner strength and beliefs
are more precious to me.
The glow of your inner self,
to my life is my guide.
I pray we're together,
as the years pass us by.
But who is to say,
what will come of this,
only a dream,
or a long-forgotten wish.
There might be a possibility,
if my freedom is obtained.
But until that day comes,
here I will remain.

**PRISONER OF LOVE**

By: Rev. Donald A. Wilson Jr.

Though time and distance separate us at this present time,
I would like you to know you are on my mind.

The love we share can transform the most common place,
into beauty, spender, sweetness and grace.

I will cherish you like I would a spring dove,
and I will always be your PRISONER OF LOVE.

**TRUE LOVE**
By: Adolph Sam

True love begins from the very first moment
two caring people meet.
Their mutual attraction shows in their eyes
and words to each other they kindly speak.

Their conversations get longer and more personal
as mutual trust slowly grows,
All day, every day, they think of each other
wherever they are and wherever they go.

True love is spending quality time together
and sharing each other's joys and pains, too.
For love means much more to me
than the erotic moments spent in bed with you.

True love gives birth to commitments
and vows we plan to keep, 'til death do us part.
Honoring them makes true love complete to me
in the deepest depths of my heart.

So when you find true love, I pray you'll realize
and tightly grab hold of it, too.
So in your old age when the worth of all else fades . . .
True love will see you through.

**SWEET SUNSHINE**
By: Adolph Sam

You fill my heart with unspeakable joy and peace,
always putting a smile on my face,
Every moment I'm blessed to see and be,
in the presence of your beauty and grace.

Storms often form with intent to destroy
my joy from day to day.
Just thinking of you, my joy's restored, and
storm's grays are blown away.

Cold winters make me shiver,
and plants start to wither,
and if forgotten, we soon will die.
Yet like a blessing from heaven,
your angel-like presence,
warms and preserves our lives.

You're so near, yet so far, and always
shining in my heart with beauty as infinite as time,
I often wonder each night and day,
will fate stay in the way
of you ever being mine,
"Sweet Sunshine."

## LOVE SHOWER

By: Levar Chung

Under the bright moon, clouds dark blue with black streaks, we spoke soul-to-soul. The heavy rain slapped the concrete spontaneously. Our body heat rose every three minutes by ten degrees. As she lay anxiously in her robe, I kissed her nose, cheeks, lips and the middle of her neck. My tongue went all over her chest. She said, "Oh." Further down her stomach, she moaned, "No-No-one but you." I gently bit her inner thighs. While shivering she said, "OOOOOH." Two moist lips I peeked and laid a kiss. She pulled my head closer. Raindrops rolled off of our bodies like dice. It felt nice. I explored inner worlds as she spilled pearls. Her eyes rolled back, tongue curled, legs and spine steady. Sensitive tip, but I was not ready. The moon blushed while she turned it into a rodeo. Then I took control. Our bodies were soaked with ecstasy. She said, "Wet me." I released and out came doves. I gave her the stars above. She kissed and bit my ear, smiled and we hugged.

## LET'S STAY TOGETHER

By: Dwayne Stephen Newson

If you say you will, I know you will
release the flames within me.
And maybe soon we both can try
to set our souls and hearts free.

When I'm alone and all is gone,
I realize you're gone, too.
So I close my eyes and wherever you are,
I find myself there with you.

Even though I promised you heaven,
I wonder, do you think of me?
Now I say I want you forever.
Will you ever leave me?

A heart of gold and spirit free,
and yet I want to chain you.
Here we are, we're both in love,
so I would not restrain you.

When we talk on the phone,
I'll always want you to know,
if you say that's where you'll be,
then that's where I will go.

Here you are inside my heart,
and there you'll stay forever.
And with my love I'll dry your tears,
and vow, let's stay together.

## NO WOMAN, NO CRY

By: Sharpe Clayton

It is what my heart holds for a woman that is very special.
Tears are held in the same manner.
As I watch an existing strength grow
that I thought would be lost in our separation,
I can only hold my head high and pray for that magic moment
when I am reunited with the woman I love.
But until then, it's *No Woman, No Cry.*
Adjusting my mind as I would a mirror.
Focusing momentarily on your beauty and the past.
I've kissed you a million times as though you were here.
But until reality is held in the palm of my hands,
it's still *No Woman, No Cry.*
I hate dealing with loose ends.
It's like a motion picture that's incomplete.
Too many emotions placed aside, and it becomes
hard to just be a man about it,
when there's *No Woman, No Cry.*

## A BRIGHTER DAY

By: Clyde Welch

I can close my eyes and see you,
hear your laughter in the air.
It only makes me miss you more
and wish I could be there.
You're out there and I'm in here
so many miles apart.
Still you linger on my mind
and live within my heart.
Even though we're miles apart,
still, somehow, we touch.
And I just wanted you to know
I love you very much.
Be strong for me, honey,
and hold your head up high.
I know it won't be easy
but baby, please don't cry.
The future's at our finger tips,
just a step away.
Right now our sky is cloudy
but we'll see a brighter day.
So you keep on, keepin' on
until our day gets here.
Remember that I love you
so baby don't you fear . . .

## TO TOUCH YOU

By: Clyde Welch

I never really took the time
to say how much I care
And right or wrong, good or bad
you were always there.
Now time has turned the pages
and you still believe in me,
out there waiting on the day
until they set me free.
I don't know what tomorrow brings
but I can tell you this:
of everyone I've ever known
you're the one I've missed.
So when I said, "I love you,"
it's because I do.
And I believe in magic
like I believe in you.
So smile for me, honey,
and things will be alright.
I love you and I miss you
and pray for you at night.
You're everything I want and need,
my every dream come true.
I'm reaching out to touch you, babe,
the way you want me to . . .

## AMBROSIA

By: Duane Anthony Brown

Who? Yes, who besides I shall partake of this potion, this elixir of the Gods?

You! Yes, you, fair maiden, come forward. You have been chosen to travel the passageways of immortality with me . . . 'tis your destiny.

Listen to me, only to me. Listen.

Drink. Drink from the cup of the arch image.
The fragrance…hypnotic, and the flavor…exotic
Drink. Drink of the cup.

It is done . . .

Radiant light! . . .an azure tint . . .we are enclosed.
We are one with all . . .undivided.

We are transformed! You . . .Aphrodite and I . . .Adonis.
We touch . . .DESIRE!

Join with me . . .COITUS! PASSION! . . .it burns through us as well as around us.
BLISS! . . .we are ethereal. Ah . . .ah . . .ECSTASY! We have created.

We are as they now…the Old Ones,
Ambrosia is our blood.

Together we have given birth to worlds . . .Utopias all.

We nourish them with our sweat. We feed them with our love.
We bathe them with our passion.

We are as they now…the Old Ones.
Ambrosia is our life force.

**LOVE IS....**
By: Richard Horton

Love has many splendors.
It has no set of rules.
Many can feel love,
intellects as well as fools.

## ETERNAL LOVE

By: Robert L. Hevlin Jr.

Eyes that shine like fine-cut diamonds;
One glance sets my heart free.
Lips softer than petals of roses
their gentle caress is my innermost plea.
Hair as silken as prized Russian sable,
as dark as the midnight Black Sea
a contrast to skin of pure alabaster.
I long for her warmth next to me.

An erudite scholar of infinite wisdom;
her mind is as crisp as the fresh morning rime.
Her beauty surpasses sweet Aphrodite's.
Her presence is stunning, her aura sublime.
A smile that rivals the smile of Venus;
one wave of her hand halts the temporal of time.
A terrestrial goddess, she's truly an angel.
She's the essence of poetry, music and rhyme.

The nymph of my dreams, we share everything.
She and I have been destined by Fate.
I've found my best friend, whom I truly adore.
In her absence nothing else sates.
A love that transcends, we've loved once before.
She and I are eternal soul mates.
She's all that I need, and I want nothing more.
Together, our future waits.

## THINKING OF YOU
By: Steven Wittman

I opened the door again, knowingly.
Knowing the pain,
and agony,
lurking,
in the shadows.

The door of sadness,
grief,
desolation,
and devastation
lay closed.
Only the brightness . . .

I willingly entered, fearless.
Forgetting the demons,
of emotions,
that accompany,
not visible
in the light.

Guard was down,
-I trusted.
Guard was down,
-I cared.
Guard was down,
-I loved.
Guard was down,
. . . I was attacked!

A broken heart mends slowly.
Such are the virtues of love.

## THE CASE OF TRUE LOVE

By: Steven Wittman

Love,
an illness that conquers reason.
Turns even the strongest man
into a….
groveling,
disgusting,
unreliable,
unpredictable,
incoherent,
weak,
piece of slime.

A virus likely to mutate and infect forever

## IMAGINE

By: Dwight E. Lewis

Imagine your life, as you desire it to be . . .
full of hope, love, life and the joy of family.
Imagine yourself riding free in the wind . . .
enjoying all of life's pleasures and then,
Imagine you and I, and how lovers should be . . .
Just close your eyes and you shall see.

The last time I saw you,
and the first time that we kissed . . .
Imagine tonight, my love, just how much you are missed.
Can you imagine at this time, holding me in your arms?
filling your heart with my love and my charms?

Close your eyes and imagine us together . . .
doing all we can, to stay lovers forever.
Our souls as one, our love is strong.
Our minds think of one another all day long.

Imagine soon, together again you and I . . .
I promise you, what I feel is not a lie.
And this important promise, I'll give to you,
my love is yours. Imagine you saying, "I do."

**IN MY DREAMS**
By: Johnny Maldonado

In this place where I must be,
laughter and joy you will never see.
Trapped forever, or so it seems, but
I escape here in my dreams.
In my dreams, I leave this place,
and hold you in a day's embrace.
Oh, how I wish I could erase
this miserable Hell without a trace.
And in my dreams I hold you near,
and all my problems disappear.
In my heart there is no fear,
a loving touch, a gentle tear.
For in my world, the birds don't sing,
this solemn world with metal rings.
The steel bars close with ghostly pings,
but I'll be with you in my dreams.

## SIX SILENT TEARS

By: Johnny Maldonado

Last night before I went to bed,
thoughts of you filled my troubled head.
Though I've not cried this way in many years,
onto my pillow fell six silent tears.
The first was for your smile that I miss,
and your tender lips that I long to kiss.
The second was for your angel face
and the thought of your warm, loving embrace.
The third came as no surprise,
I thought of your beautiful, blue eyes.
After this the fourth came rolling.
Instead of my pillow, it was you I should've been holding.
The fifth came for one reason alone,
I felt my love for you was not fully shown.
I really miss you, my dear.
There at last fell the sixth silent tear.

**ENCHANTRESS**
By: Ronald Hutton

As I drift amongst the corridors of my Soul,
I dream . . .

I am engulfed in the many visions of you
that dance before my "tightly closed eyes."

I remain "overwhelmed by your presence . . ."
your Love
flowing over me,
like soft cool water from a stream
that arises out of nothingness.

Bathed in your Love, I feel your gentle loving hands
as they touch my Soul . . .
as they cup and cradle my Heart.

"If only I were able to touch you in this way . . ."

"Aware of your cares my spirit soars to become one
with yours," to unite in the Heavens . . .
a mystical union long forgotten in the lore of ancient past.

As we close the door on our past, another opens . . .
Exposing the brightness of our future together . . .

And I find myself "forever in your debt."

## THE QUEST ENDS

By: Donald E. Tennyson

When I think of happiness, love and joy
I picture a woman:
mature, yet coy.
with beautiful features and strength of mind.
This is the person,
I long to find.
I've searched and searched, endured sadness and pain
for at the end of each quest
I sit alone and ashamed.
Now as I ponder my freedom it seems,
the person I long for
will remain just a dream.

**WEDDING DAY**
By: Robert R. Martin

Early Sunday morning with a light rain falling,
a gentle wind carries the church bell's calling.
People gather inside and each take their place.
The preacher is at the pulpit, a smile on his face.

There is a beautiful lady with eyes so bright.
They shine like stars on a clear winter's night.
She walks down the aisle gracefully, like a queen.
A more beautiful woman, there is none to be seen.

Before the smiling preacher, the couple stands.
I heard the old feller say, "Please join hands."
Everybody is happy as they all begin to sing,
while on her finger, he places a wedding ring.

Yes, my friends, a lifetime dream has come true
with a future ever so bright and gay.
For two people who are deeply in love,
are happily married today.

## LOVE CONQUERS

By: Nathaniel Hamilton

I am a fighter by nature and refuse to lose in any situation,
but you are my toughest battle yet.
Nothing will tame me, for I shall do as I please.
But you are much more dangerous than I expected.
So I must be very careful not to slip
and lose myself within your depths.
Cautiously, I ease into your vast and open sea
for only one of us can win.
And suddenly . . . there is nothing for me to hold onto
and now I must swim without direction
If I do not, I will surely drown.
You are so warm and inviting
breaking down my barriers of resistance.
Caressing and soothing
tempting, fierce and powerful with your luring eyes.
I know now, that I will never control your actions or will.
Farther I am pulled into the center of your void.
Suddenly afraid, I panic, struggling to stay as I am.
I must not, cannot surrender
for you are more than I can bare.
But still, I am drowning . . .
and you will not free me from your will, forcing me
to give up my chance to see things as I always do.
No one will save me.
I am doomed to sink even farther within your depths, lost to myself,
never existing or functioning as my normal self again.
You are truly unexpected, so determined in your ways.
And wave after wave crashes upon my heart, blending me,
mixing my existence with yours.
I surrender only because I am drowning,
drowning in your sea of love.

**THE BEAUTIFUL YOU**
By: Larry L. Belle

I began these words of beauty with a dearness I give to me.
Concerning your "beauty,"
your rays of "love," your epitome,
things I feel; yet cannot see.
Your beauty I feel and feelings that I get
with sufficient consideration, gracefully persists.
I've embraced your beauty as a gift from above.
I've embraced it as a token of "love."
I feel the piercing of eyes that sparkle with intellect,
capturing my entirety with scintillating effects;
effects, that are "prodigious," promising, and "true,"
bringing out the truest essence of how I feel about you.
Your beauty crossed lines of boundaries,
which says you'll face a dare.
Your beauty says that life has treated you fair.
Your beauty is in essence, the souls of you and me.
A part of salvation, your beauty made me free.
Your beauty is intrinsic, accompanied by magical ends,
forcing the gritting of teeth; yet giving me strength to bend.
Your beauty restored in me harmony seemed forever lost.
Your beauty possesses might; you shared in the cost.
Your beauty is so real I can't think of it enough.
It sheltered me from the cold when my entirety wasn't enough.
Your beauty has given to me a tendency to incline.
Your beauty you shared with me; leaving me willing to share what's mine;
It told me to stay strong to cope and not take risks.
It fixes my broken heart with happiness and bliss.
Your beauty's all I've listed that and much more.
It noticed me off course and brought me back to shore.
Your beauty all that's beautiful I've lived and found that true.
That's why these words of beauty are titled:
"The Beautiful You."

## PAIN AND HAPPINESS

By: Miko D. Smith

So much pain in this world, so little happiness
Is it true that after I leave this oh, horrible world,
I will feel bliss?
'Cause if it's true, I'm ready to leave now,
if I can't feel your touch,
your beautiful face.
I just love you so much.
My poems to you are true and from my heart.
It breaks me up, 'cause we are so far apart.
I could never find the courage
to express my feelings for you.
But I want you to know that my love for you is true.
Forever and always you are in my heart,
to be my girl, my boo, even my eyes to see.
It probably trips you out, the things that I write.
But I have to let you know, since I am out of sight.
Things between you and I will be different with my return,
'cause when I come home, my love for you will still burn.
But until I am back, try not to be so blue,
'cause, baby girl, I will always love you!

## A COMING DAY

By: Steven J. Anderson

As shadows fall on another day done,
the last few rays from a setting sun.
One day closer, but still far away,
freedom, I'll find on that coming day.

As darkness gathers, unknowing prevails.
An emptiness growing, my personal hell
What was before can never be,
Only one to blame and that is me.

Surrounded by memories, good and bad.
Smiles of joy, the love we had.
The past won't change the anger and pain.
Forgiveness must come, a cleansing rain.

So many times love was pushed away,
So many times lost, what we had to say.
The words were so easy, but never said,
They haunt me nightly within my head.

Now the greatest fear that I carry around,
is the silence between us, not even a sound.
For love is not quiet, of that I am sure,
the heartbeats of love so sweet and pure.

I live through these nightly, visiting fears,
remembering your touch that I hold so dear,
afraid I might be what the future holds,
but a destiny awaits, a story untold.

So whenever you watch the setting sun,
remember the love that can't be undone.
A new day is coming and that I await,
I pray you will be there, forever my mate.

As darkness flees from a sky deep blue,
These words will echo: "I love you!"

# Families, Untied

## THE UNEXPECTED GIFT

By: Zena Y. Long

I sat there staring at her loving face, looking into her precious, hazel eyes. Her tiny, plump, little fingers were wrapped around my shaking index finger. I silently stared at her, tears swelling in my eyes. This was to be the very last time to feel her tender newborn skin upon my own. I wanted to remember her adoring smile and her look of angelic beauty. The little bubbles appeared on the tips of her tiny rosy lips when she exhaled. Her darkened strands of tiny hair curled around her little baby ears. I wanted to remember the tender look of my precious daughter.

I sat there intently studying her while my mind raced through my promiscuous past. This was the only hope for a better life for my beautiful baby girl. I made myself believe that what I was doing was right. This was the last option for me, the only right thing to do. A tear fell from my face and landed on the front porch where my child and I sat for our last time. I moved to touch my innocent beauty to remember her warmth and softness. Everything in me wanted to pick her up and run like hell. Just run away and live a life with her by my side. But I knew in my heart that I couldn't adequately provide the necessities a healthy child needs. As my tears stung my eyes I found the strength to whisper my final words to my newborn baby girl. "I love you. This is the best I can do. I know these people will be loving and able to provide a better life for you, my precious baby girl." As I whispered I could see my breath caress my daughter's chilled rosy cheeks. I had to do this before she became too cold or became sick. I undid my little girl's plump fingers from my own and tucked her pink cotton blanket around her tiny body. I gently tugged on her tiny little pink knit cap to be sure her head was as warm as possible. As I tenderly kissed her on her soft, cold cheeks, my eyes stung and my heart ached for her. Picking up her car seat I whispered, "I love you" for my last time. I propped the car seat up against the wooden door and took my final glance at my innocent baby.

I rang the doorbell and hurried down the cement steps. I ran down the dark street with tears pouring from my eyes and my heart torn forever. As I ran I never looked back, never looking back to the only house with a porch light on in the dark, deserted street.

# LIFE BEHIND BARS

By: David Wayne Nelson

Prison is a monster that slowly eats away your soul.
Love is quickly changed to hate then the monster proudly plays his role.

Society doesn't see what goes on behind these man-made gates of Hell.
They think prison life is rosy but the facts of horror are hidden well.

Some people do belong in prison and some of them even deserve to die.
But some are here for lack of money or as a victim of someone else's lie.

I know what prison can do. I've seen warm, kind hearts turn to stone.
I've watched men slowly die inside searching for hope that's long been gone.

Visits from loved ones are special, but Sundays seem years apart.
And some Sundays never come. Forgetting shells, existing with a broken heart.

Family and friends often forget you and at mail call you can see the pain
But each day they listen and pray hoping the mailman will call their name.

Some of my best friends I met in prison, and in here, friends are rare.
But one true friend in here is worth all the ones out there.

## A BLESSING IN DISGUISE:
### A Tribute To Mother
By: Kevin L. Evans

*You* have been there since the beginning. *You* were the vessel in which I was delivered to this physical life.

When I was but an infant, I looked to you for protection, and for instruction, substance and direction. Yes! My mother, you have always been there. Even now when it seems that the rest of the world as I know it has *slammed* its doors in my face, and has literally, thrown-away the key. Still you are here, never giving up on me.

In what appears to be my "Darkest Hour," it is you who battles the in climate weather to ensure that I have a familiar face to look upon periodically. With all your burdens, you still manage to "stow-away" some extra time just for me, even if it's just to answer my collect long-distance telephone calls. With all that you do, I often forget to thank you. Lots of times, as a result of my own misery, I make it seem like I don't appreciate you. Only then, after being alone with my conscience, do I realize how very *blessed* I am to have you.

Just so that you know, you are a "Blessing In Disguise," Mother. You are *highly* appreciated and so *desperately* needed. Thank you for not giving up on me, after all of these years! I would also like for you to realize that you are in so many ways my "Pillar of Strength." This subtle tribute has awakened that part of me that I often *fight* to subdue for fear of showing my immense affection for you to others. If not for you, this trying time, being locked-away, could have very easily driven me, "over the edge of sanity's cliff." While I have you with me, I promise to begin taking a "closer look" at whose care and concern for me "outshines" all the rest.

**Thank You, Mother, for your continued support, love and affection.**

Your Son,
Kevin

## A FATHER'S LOVE

By: Joshua Aaron Wiltfong

A father's love
is like no other.
He mends up wounds
and tucks in covers.

He would give his life
to save his child.
His touch is gentle
and his words are mild.

He watches her grow
throughout the years.
He would give anything
if she never had to shed any tears.

I see you in your pictures
as beautiful as a dove.
I'm sorry; I'm not there
to show you a father's love.

## THANK YOU

By: Joshua Aaron Wiltfong

Thank you for not leaving.
Thank you for being strong,
When I did right,
or when I did wrong.

You're a very special Mother
with nerves of steel.
You always helped me out
no matter what the deal.

I wish I were there
to thank you in person.
But I'll be there soon, Mom,
of that, I'm certain.

## MY DAUGHTER, MONE'

By: J. A. Banks (Nantambu)

Star child's
morning sunshine
captures my heart.

As the dawn overtakes
darkness of night,
shine upon me those love rays
as I walk these nomadic days.

When thought becomes cold,
misty blue . . .without you
only a void exists.

For time never fills these
empty days of roller coaster rides,
of feelings unsatisfied.

My star child
morning sunshine
precious Mone'
meet me at this place
called . . .love.

**A FATHER'S LOVE**
By: Aaron Lamar Sampson

I'm telling you this because I love you.
I pray to the Lord you can understand.
I know I'm not much of a father
Sometimes, I'm not much of a man.

In life we must make decisions.
Some are not always right.
My choice to abandon you and your mother
has kept me crying many nights.

I have no right to lecture you
or offer fatherly advice
but if you listen closely to what I say,
it just may save your life.

The penitentiary is not hereditary
nor is it your destiny.
Ignore the popular trail.
Make your own path; that's the key.

You bring out the best in me. I wish you knew that.
I'm sorry for all I've done.
Maybe I can show you a different me
to help you later in life, when raising your son

If you apply yourself and define yourself
I assure you, you can succeed.
I plan to take my own advice
and be the father that you need.

Generations before you
the penitentiary has claimed
I fought the battle and lost.
It's up to you, my son, to break the chains.

I promise to work harder.
Never again will you be neglected.
A father's love is here for you
if you are willing to accept it.

## THE QUESTION

By: Edward Armstrong

*To birth or not to birth?*
A question every woman must face.
The changes that a child will bear upon her fate
Yet, Mother, you chose to bring this life into the world.
Trusting in the goodness of God,
you offered this world your pearl.
Still, there were many nights
when your eyes overflowed with tears.
Trusting despite disappointments,
believing, despite your fears.
Your love continued to grow
as your wisdom became my guide.
And eventually, the pearl you offered
will become your joy and pride.
I know my choices were often wrong
and my decisions often poor,
but the mistakes that have branded my past
are mine, not yours.
You have done all that you can do,
and in all things provided the best.
Yet the life that you created
must struggle through its own test.
I thank you for all you've done to prepare me for this earth
And I am grateful that the answer to your question was indeed,
"TO BIRTH."

## THE JOY OF LIFE

By: Darryl Payne

As morning broke, light began to filter in through his bars. He stretched, and once again took notice of his surroundings. Facing yet another day in prison, his first thought was, "I wish that I was dead, then all this would be over."

When he glanced out of his window, his eyes caught the glory of the morning's sunrise, majestic in its splendor. He breathed in and out while standing at his window and caught the scent of blossoms from the spring trees. Hungry, he took a bite from an apple saved from last night's dinner, sweet and wet as only a firm, deep, red apple can be. While changing clothes, he momentarily stopped to feel the texture of his pajamas. Although they weren't expensive or outwardly special, the feel reminded him of loved ones back home who sent them, Jackie and the kids. On the radio, that old Impression's song was playing, "Keep on Pushin'," with its message of inspiration and working it through and towards another day.

Once again, his five senses had reminded him of just how wonderful it was to be alive.

## RUSSIAN MOTHER'S CRY

By: Fredrick D. Howell

Russian mothers cry this day
for sons now lost at sea,
swallowed by the oceans depths,
their tomb, a submarine.
Sisters, brothers, mothers, fathers, wives
weep silently for those they love,
hanging onto one last thread of hope,
silent prayers to God above.
Pleas for help now from nearby allies
they know may have come too late,
all because of foolish pride
Hands of power hold their fate.
For they know if no one can reach them soon
to pluck them from the ocean floor,
the light of another day they'll never see,
their voices silenced forevermore.
So I say this prayer for them all tonight
for they are my fellowmen,
to the Father of us, one and all,
who hears our prayers and understands.
Sweet Jesus, up in heaven above
I ask this in your name,
that you watch over these lost loved ones.
Please don't let them die in vain.
If it is your will, Lord,
please return them to their mother's loving arms.
Safely place them in Your hands.
Shield these children from all harm.
Comfort all their families, Father,
who are waiting for their safe return.
And Lord, dry the tears this day
of that "Russian mother's cry". . .

## KATHY SUE

By: David W. Davis

Sweet is the time,
I spend thinking of you,
The times we have shared,
the trials we've been through.
Now I haven't seen you,
in long, lonely years.
And you can believe,
there's been anguish and tears.
Yet those days, those are past,
I can never retrieve.
But as for our future,
I shall pray and believe.

## ONE WISH

By: James C. Johnson Jr.

If I had one wish, I would wish for enormous wealth,
and help the children who are poor.
That is what I would wish for myself.
I wish that something would happen for the good.
I wish drugs and violence
did not live in our neighborhoods.
I wish I could do more things to help
people than I have done.
I wish I could have been a better
friend and father to my son.
But my wishes, it seems, are based on things I dream.
I hope to one day make them come true.
That's why I express these wishes to you.
There's one more thing I wish,
and I wish this for all people to see.
Every wish that I have made,
I made these wishes for you and me.

## THE GIFT OF A FRIENDSHIP
By: John Maldonado

Friendship is a priceless gift,
that cannot be bought or sold.

But its value is far greater,
than a mountain made of gold.

'Cause gold is cold and lifeless,
it cannot see or hear.

And in time, when you are troubled,
it is powerless to cheer.

It has no ears to listen, and
no heart to understand.

It cannot bring you comfort,
or reach out a helping hand.

So when you ask God for a gift,
be thankful if he sends,

Not diamonds, gold or riches,
but the love of a true friend.

## MOTHER AND FATHER

By: Joseph Yoder

Mother: I appreciate the love you've shown
and how you've always cared for me.
For when I was down, I was never alone
because you were always there for me.
I may not say it enough and try to act tough
but sometimes, you must put pride aside.
You're my mother who I love, who has been sent from above
and that's truly from deep down inside.

Father: Over the years and through all the tears
and laughing and life that you've lived,
you've soared like an eagle, been strong like a bear.
Thank you for the cheer that you give.
As long as the geese migrate to the east
or north or wherever they go,
I will always love you in my heart.
You'll stay true and that I just want you to know.

## COME FORTH

By: David W. Davis

Gentle breezes caressing,
warm as sweet thoughts of home,
bringing forth memories peacefully.
'Tis a comfort for I'm so alone,
so alone in this sea of faces.
Strangers who all know my name,
I allow them to know whom to blame.
Come forth! Come forth, one who loves me.
Emerge from this liquid confusion,
a soul to love and to care for,
where my presence shall not be an intrusion.

## 37c AFFAIR

By: Rodney Edwards

As I sit within this city of brick, steel and stone,
I frantically wait for the mailman to come along.
As I observed an officer coming my way,
he clearly said, “There’s no mail for you today.”
Frustrated,
disappointed,
and still trying to understand,
why day after day he never has any mail for me
in his mother-fucking hand.
I almost snapped when I jumped in his face.
He simply said, “You can’t trip with me. Get on your woman’s case.”
His words penetrated deep within my mind.
So the next letters I sent contained these lines . . .
“I know you are very compassionate and ever so sweet.
Would you consider writing me a letter sometime this week?
Because I’m quite sure there are a few words you can openly share.
Especially when not too long ago,
you led me to believe you truly cared.
It’s bad enough I’m deprived of my freedom
within this sad and lonely prison camp.
But what hurts so much is finding out
the relationship that I value dearly,
doesn’t have the value of a 37c stamp!”

## IT'S ALL BUT OVER . . .

By: Steven Wittman

When I see myself
through your eyes;
the image isn't
as bright,
as brilliant,
as pleasing
as before.

The reflection is dim,
sad,
displeasing
to the soul . . .

My spirit cries for realignment.

## THE KNIGHT

By: Steven J. Anderson

I close my eyes and drift away,
a floating leaf on a windy day
I call your name within my mind,
a comfort, I seek, but do not find.
For reality rears its ugly head.
The past is gone; the past is dead.
Like forgotten toys: a wagon red,
a rusted bike deep in a shed
a puppy once, but now all grown,
things you cherished, but now all thrown
into the corner just out of sight,
all growing dusty in the dim, dull light.
Cobwebs growing of broken dreams,
remembered not, it now does seem.
Happiness and laughter are echoing cries.
There's nothing left but meaningless lies.
Once I was needed to slay your dragons,
forgotten now with the little red wagon.
Forever I'll be in the dawn's first light,
the one you may need, your shining knight.
So when that time comes, just give a call,
I'll be there to catch you when you fall.

# ABSENT, BUT NOT FORGOTTEN

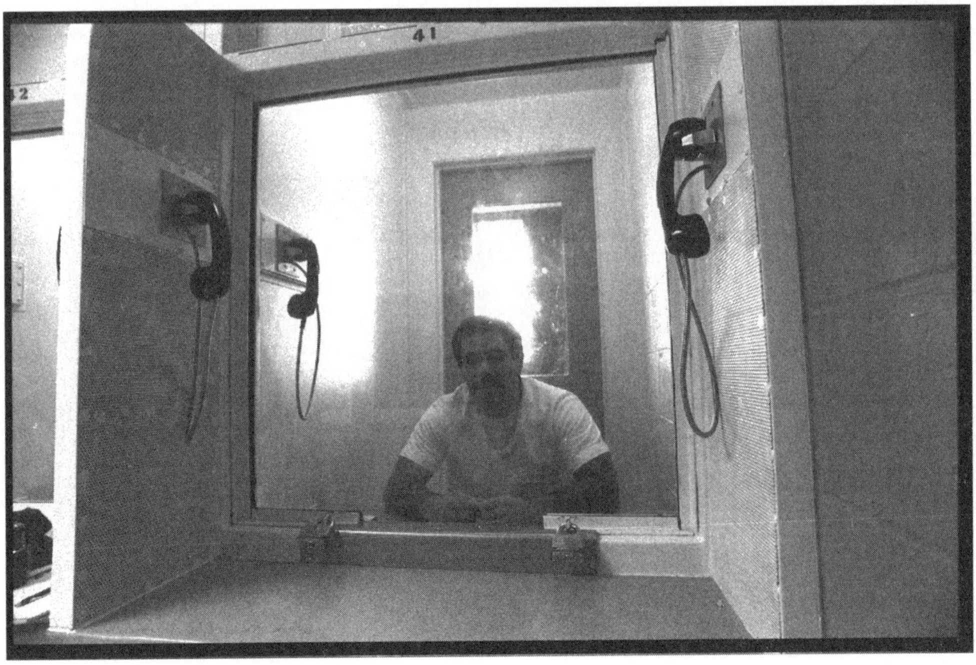

## CRADLE TO THE CHAIR

By: Leroy E. Jacobs

When I left home, I told Mama
someday, I'd return
and I'd have riches that she
could keep or burn.
But the road that I traveled
got too hard for me to bear.
And it's a *long*, *long* way from the cradle
to the darkness of the chair

I met a man in a bar room.
I was hungry. Lord, I was cold.
And for one drink of wine
I sold my soul.
We got into a fight.
A stranger lay dying there.
And it's a *long*, *long* way from the cradle
to the darkness of the chair

Well mama, tonight this letter
comes to you from death-row
and it'll be the last letter I ever write,
'cause tomorrow, they'll take my life.
Hey, come on now, Mama; please don't cry
It's not your fault. All your life
you and Dad really did try
As my mind goes back in time
I can see you now,
back home in those old cotton fields,
that sun beating down
and the sweat, just dripping from your brow.

Lord knows, Mama,
I wish I could be there
to take that load off your back.
But I know again,
I'll never be there . . .
'Cause it's a *long*, *long* way from the cradle
to the darkness of the chair
Yes, it's a *long*, *long* way from the cradle
to the darkness of the chair,
Good-bye, Mama . . .

## SUMMER RAIN
**(In the memory of Cassie Rogers and Cris Rousley)**

By: Aaron Lamar Sampson

Sometimes I can smell the rain
even before it falls.

Sometimes I can sense an upcoming storm
while everything around me is calm.

Sometimes I can hear a whisper
flowing softly through the air.

I see a forgotten smile,
but when I open my eyes there's no one there.

Sometimes I catch that brief scent,
time spent thinking back.

I realize things will never be the same,
it's just hard to accept that fact.

Sometimes I can smell the rain,
even before it makes a sound.

It reminds me of every emotion
that has been buried in the ground.

## I AM, THEREFORE I DIE

By: Kenneth Campbell

Through my many years of wandering
nothing ever was found.
The dreams that I was searching for
lie shattered on the ground

An odyssey of yesterday's
traveled only in my mind.
Nothing can separate us
from the memories left behind.

I was born and I grew up
much like others seemed to be.
So, where is the one to tell me
was it "I" or destiny?

Soon the questions will have their answers
as to what, and where, and why,
for tomorrow I escape the net.
As a bird, my soul will fly

Would you like me if you knew me?
Is there any feeling there?
This is all I have to say,
I go now to the chair . . .

## EMPATHY FOR AN EXECUTION

By: Daniel Manning

A current of silent sorrow
passes through me.
A misery
that is everywhere,
unseen.
My feelings, small
yet significant
in the silence,
as the silence was like an immense scream.
The pain was blurring my vision.
Seeing strange images
that weren't my own.
Faces full of anguish
with their own choking cries.
All beyond this violation
that I have always known.
My grief is rising
including all losses in life.
And so in dark obscurity
it comes to this . . .
All I have to do is
sink deeper inside myself
to suffer through this emptiness.

Within the depths of my soul
a thought rings out like a voice . . .
In oblivion we are forgiven all things.

## CAPTURED MOMENTS

By: Steven York Lent

Warm afternoon, I feel the rain
coming down between the sun and moon.
As the earth keeps spinning 'round
the clouds play atop the air,
and all I do is stare as I'm stuck here
upon the ground.
In line, out of touch, don't really
need that much.
My expressions try and view
You'll see nothing new
I'm only lost within the laughter,
surprised all the day after
by the faces of the few
inside and out, what's it all about?
Silent breeze across the sky,
there is dust in my eye.
Speechless as the second day rushes by,
another way, confused and often too high
In tune, out of time; just want to find a
reason why these captured moments just go by.

**THE REAL**
By: David W. Davis

Forty years I've walked this Earth,
A survivor, I know not how.
I know for sure there is a plan
divine that has led me to now.
I write this in a prison cell,
more free than on the street.
In my past, a captive for sure,
mistakes did I repeat.

## THE HUMAN EXPERIENCE

By: David W. Davis

Trapped within this bottle,
this vessel made of clay,
hardens until it turns to dust,
from the heat throughout the day.

## YESTERDAY'S KISS

By: Robin A. Kephart

She said to write. Just pick up your pen and begin. It doesn't matter what spills out the end, it only matters that whatever is there does. So, I began, just that way. I pulled the paper from the folder, two sheets, and laid them at a slant on the table in front of me. I picked up the pen and began. The following was heard in the silence within when I listened that day:

I start here in this single moment in time to reflect on the past. I see it there amidst the fog of so many memories. The days I left behind, so many years ago. I can feel the sun on my head, warming my hair as it splashes from the sky. There is safety in the sun. Somehow, it always seems that way. The light creates gentleness for the world and holds it against her breast, rocks it back and forth in her peace. The grass beneath my feet feels cool and the smell of a new summer dances around the air. Do I honestly remember being this alive? So alive that the world around me sang and I could hear the melody in all the sounds that came forth?

Where is my soul now? I sense it still, stirring restlessly behind some dark wall of stone. I call out but all that comes back to me is the echo of my own voice in the stillness. I sit amidst the blackness and weep for the little girl that I can no longer find.

My mind wanders to all the forgotten forevers ago and I lift my eyes to a picture of a beautiful place. It's a cottage, nestled amidst a cluster of trees. It is quiet there. I can hear the quiet as it whispers, chatting endlessly with the emptiness surrounding it. So, I step forward and feel the soft warm wind kiss my cheek in welcome. I am home.

I walk toward the door, I know the way without really seeing for I've visited this place many times in the forgotten dreams of the past. My hand reaches to turn the knob and as I grasp it, I feel happy for no particular reason. I push gently and step into yesterday, and then suddenly I stop, taken by surprise for a moment. Confusion is licking at my heels. I left the present to find the past, stopped in a dream of tomorrow and now find myself somewhere in between. The pictures on the wall portray a life, a life that was, as it shifted and changed, what was meant to be.

A child laughing danced in a field of flowers in the first portrait and waved as she tumbled into the grass and out of sight. I knew those eyes and the laughter they held and for a moment, I remembered, but only for a moment.

The next frame showed a summer afternoon in an old schoolroom. She sat at a desk, beneath an open window. The smell of freshly cut grass softly crept in with the wind, carrying the warmth of a promise held in her heart. It surrounded me and I shivered as its fingers caressed my skin. She lifted her pencil and began writing her dreams, as the teacher lectured on about history and how it evolved. She was lost in what would be, not today, but someday.

My eyes roamed to the next scene, a red frame this time. I see a young woman and the isle on which she stood. Paved with precious jewels in an array of color, the isle sparkled like a brilliant gleam of hope. Her gown was white, and the tassel on her cap swayed, though she stood so very still. I watched the pictures on the wall behind her change, portraying a life that had not yet been lived, yet beckoning with each new scene a purpose so full it burst with vitality that lit up the room. She stood like a princess engulfed in the light that created an aura around her. A hand reached for hers, and as she took it and stepped forward, she paused, turned my way, and winked (no one noticed that wink but me, and I understood).

I turned the corner to search for the final picture. I walked down a dark hallway until I saw a soft glow illuminating from the wall, and there I stopped. She sat on a rock by a quiet stream and in her hands she held a broken heart. I looked at her eyes, but the film of sadness that covered them dried up the sparkle of life that should have been there.

I knelt before this last painting and watched. She rocked back and forth so slowly, as she cradled the broken heart so gently in her arms. There was a lullaby floating out from her mouth and the melody ripped at my soul. "Where did you go?" I screamed at the painting. "Where did you go?"

She was my inner child, you know, the part of my life that found pleasure in the flowers, the part that could feel the music when she danced, the part that understood how to love. She was the part that had died.

Behind me, I heard the cries again, but I could not move. I could not turn for somewhere deep inside I knew I could never get back to the other side. Somehow, I knew that no matter how much I wanted to hold her again, she would no longer exist for me. I rose slowly and backed away. The agony of knowing would now curse me as I walked toward the end of my road. Like a bad dream, it would haunt me forever, whispering in my ear, "She was a gift, a precious gift, and you didn't save her. Now she has been taken from it." I closed my eyes and let my journey continue. When the time came to open them again, I would be somewhere else, and just maybe the sun would shine there, just maybe . . .

## I'LL BE THERE

By: Steven J. Anderson

As the setting sun slowly slips away,
a gentle breeze born at the end of the day
a bright new moon on an evening fair.
You close your eyes and I'll be there.

Sparkling stars blanket the sky,
tears from the moon as he silently cries.
He looks upon you, wind in your hair,
Just close your eyes and I'll be there.

Separated by distance though close by heart,
I miss you so much; it tears me apart.
I fall to my knees with a silent prayer.
Just close your eyes and I'll be there.

The pain that you carry, just give it to me.
I'll shoulder it gladly and let you be free.
If there was a way to show I care,
Just close your eyes and I'll be there.

Your fears are arrows that strike me deep,
shot from the heavens, God's own keep.
When you awake with terrible nightmares,
Just close your eyes and I'll be there.

A day is coming; I promise you'll see.
Happiness you'll find as it used to be.
To be alone will be very rare,
When you open your eyes, I'll be there!

## THE LAST SUNRAYS

By: Steven J. Anderson

No words alone can fully explain,
the fear in neither my heart nor its pain.
Like a slowly, tightening, constricting vise,
the warmth inside fades to ice.

No longer are colors so enticingly bright,
suddenly faded to a dull gray light.
The joy of awakening to a summer day,
gone as I await the last sunrays.

In darkness, I seek a comfort unreal.
In silence alone, with that I can deal.
Meaningless chatter from a distance, I hear.
Deaf to the world, it seems, I fear.

I delve into my mind, a world unknown.
All battles are fought in there, alone.
I carry a smile, fake that it be,
a masquerade, up front, for all to see.

Learning to use my eyes to hide,
the feelings and thoughts hidden inside.
Then late at night the echoes are back,
the memories they bring, in my wall, a crack.

As though dying of thirst, of these, I drink,
a time of joy, my sanity's last link.
So darkness is now the crutch I need,
good times of the past, the book I read.

Now I mount my dreams, some galloping nightmares.
Ride through the darkness through traps and liars.
Though worn and weary by the coming day,
I'll wait once more for the last sunrays.

## CLOUD-SHADOWED MOUNTAINS

By: Robert Raymond Martin

I was walking along the top of a mountain looking at the rays of the sun as they beamed down through the branches of the great and beautiful trees. In the distance, clouds of grayish white cast their shadows across slopes and valleys of the magnificent forests that covered the land for miles and miles around.

I thought about how free and wonderful it must feel to be able to fly, to fall with the wind beating my face, tearing my clothes and pulling me up, even though I was falling down, but never to touch the ground, only the casting of my shadow as I fly over the vast wilderness.

I stopped to study a small creek as it splashed and jumped over rocks and treetops that were laying in and around the small stream, flowing so lovely away from everything to nowhere. Here it is today, but where will it be tomorrow? Only the water would know or care . . .

I could see and hear small birds and animals of all kinds as they played where birds and animals have played for millions of years. They seem to be happy with what they have, never complaining, never looking for anything better. They just come and go over the endless seasons of endless time . . .

Big trees, little trees, all the trees that have gone and those yet to come, all different kinds reach for what everything is reaching for, the sky, but not quite making it. Still, they grow and grow as big as they possibly can, just to fall with death where it all began. I walked over small and large rocks with little clusters of brown, blue and green moss laying on and around them, through freshly bloomed wildflowers, through knee-high grass and leaves dry with the brittle sound of burning wood . . .

I walked out on a high cliff overlooking as far as the eye could see. I knew I was standing on top of everything that was wonderful and beautiful, all that was good and bad, happiness and sadness, life and death. I was a part of something no words can or could ever describe. As I fell, I thought of how the wind beat my face and tore not at my clothes but at my life. Right then I knew the Kingdom of God, as He and I flew over cloud-shadowed mountains . . .

**FEBRUARY MORN**
By: Keith A. Luecke

Oh, the dawn of another day within this dreary time of year
The gray clouds of February morn in which there is no cheer

For most, when we think to look up, brings a sense of encouragement and hope
But to look up at that dull, dreary sky, brings me nothing but despair and I can't cope.

Oh, sun, when will you ever shine? Oh, sky, when will you ever clear?
Heaven's blue I wish to fill my eye, rather than this lonesome, solitary tear.

This day, it happens every year when I again must acknowledge my birth
To look at my failures and my fears and wish to escape the bonds of earth

Oh, February morn, why do you haunt me so? Why must you come again?
Before next year, please, just let me go, I am ready for life in Heaven to begin.

**MY INSPIRATION**
By: Darryl L. Proffit

The people who made a way for us inspire many of us. They set the examples for those who may choose to follow. I recognize one person in particular for his skills and contributing factors. His name is Sidney Poitier.

Sidney Poitier grew up on the Cat Island of the Bahamas. The actor made the journey to the United States and arrived with only three dollars ($3.00) in his pockets.
He then became one of New York's finest dishwashers. He was a man with minimal education, but a maximized sense of self. He listened to the radio for long hours to get rid of his Caribbean accent. He also began a long process of intense self-education through reading. He volunteered at the American Negro Theater as a janitor in exchange for acting lessons. He then became one of Hollywood's greatest actors.

Briefly, I will describe how this great actor overcame diversity and established himself as a unique performer. Mr. Poitier subverted the racial stereotypes of old Hollywood by portraying strong, resolute and intelligent characters in a range of movies from "Cry, The Beloved Country" to "A Raisin In The Sun" (1951-1961). In these major Hollywood films, he portrayed roles such as doctors, teachers, lawyers and other achievement-oriented professionals.

I am greatly moved by this actor's determination and accomplishments. He has shown us that we, too, can change our lives if we work hard and dedicate ourselves. His life story exemplifies the fact that we, too, can break the barriers that suppress our thoughts in achieving our goals. He had made me an admirer of his work and has given me inspiration.

**UNSEEN ORCHESTRA**
By: Celia Reynolds

While searching for something else
I came upon a saxophone.
Stumbling through life, the brassy gleam
caught my eye, it shined
just in the nick of time.
New to my hands,
the weight was odd,
But it felt as though
between by palms
lay an unborn child.
Out of curiosity
I raised the metal to my mouth
and met it with unfamiliar lips,
caressed the keys with the first finger prints
From the first breath
my lungs and lips
gave birth to song.
Without tripping over a treble clef,
out came a pure and perfect melody
In all the confusion,
a musical ecstasy.
From somewhere in my soul,
a wind blew,
and I composed.
It brought tears to my dry eyes.
It put a smile on my tired face.
I played the song that plays in me,
I heard the notes . . .
*And I was free.*

# Living Life ...
# ...With Time

**TIME**

By: Steven Wittman

*Drip*,
Another day,
  *Drip,*
  *Drip,*
  *Drip*,
  Another week.
    *Drip,*
    *Drip,*
    *Drip*
    *Drip*
    *Drip,*
    Another year . . . the hollow *drip* of the soul.

  Time gives way, meaningless,
  Meaningless ways give time.

  Spirit fights desolation,
  Condensation of happiness,
  From the shell . . . . . . . . . . . . *Drips*,
          Another day.
          *Drip,*
          *Drip*,
          *Drip*,
          Another week.
            *Drip,*
            *Drip,*
            *Drip*
            *Drip*
            *Drip,*
            Another . . .

**SAME OLD, SAME OLE**
By: Sharon White

I get up in the morning
and start preparing for the day,
waiting to hear the breakfast call
in the same old, same ole way.

It's 8:05, and time to go
to catch up with the line.
I grab my coat and head for the door
at the same old, same ole time.

At 3:25, my job is done.
I wait for the bell to ring.
I take my bag, say goodbye
doing the same old, same ole thing.

Back to where I started from
it feels like it's all a waste,
doing the same things over and over
in this same old, same ole place.

## WINGS

By: J. A. Banks (Nantambu)

Traveling does not
always depend
upon our feet.
Sometimes just sitting
miles will meet.

Overlooking barriers
that block with ease
flowing rivers
ocean water
open seas

Traveling with waves
likewise inside caves
Walls that crack, then crumble,
Silent journeys that make us strong yet, humble

Exiting in pathways
with light-bending rays
Exploring minds behind doors
traveling
with wings that soar, hoping to . . .

**ESCAPE**

By: J. A. Banks (Nantambu)

Release those chains
from the entangled thoughts
that confine them with confusion
before falling into an abyss

Hopelessly drifting,
devoid of visions
tranquilized by
misconceptions of life
for bondage has captured . . .

## ANOTHER UNIVERSE

By: J. A. Banks (Nantambu)

Their minds, while casting
physical images of freedom
why is it quaint to think,
forms aside,
that fear is comfort secured?

Beyond a dream to be free
sheltered in shackles
hidden within closets
thinking you're safe
and they're gone

They exist, blind-folded.
You are linked to death
with dry tears of pain
and persuaded to believe
that this is destiny's fix

Seemingly aware
yet, unable to behold
that reality doesn't mix
while living
in a world of dreams.
Inclined to escape
from the dark place
once with painted faith
and prayers without change

Exploding and unleashing
yet, another universe
composed so bright;
realizing that the cage
never was but a mind
devoid of light

**YOU**

By: Sharon White

Like an arrow through my heart,
you pierced my being.
The thief who robbed me of my joy,
I KNOW YOU.

Although, I saw no face
you are not colorless,
for I feel your blackness.
I CAN IDENTIFY YOU.

You are not welcome here
yet, you continue to stay.
I can no longer live with you inside.
PLEASE . . . JUST GO AWAY!

You're the phantom that never leaves my side . . .

**GRIEF**

## CITY OF THE DEAD

By: Robert L. Hevlin Jr.

They gnaw at one's flesh in this cinder from Hell,
the Imps and the Trolls who inhabit this pail.

They shrill and they screech in an unbridled way,
while consuming one's mind with each passing day.

It's a loathsome abyss with its gruesome despair,
filled with devils and demons and their faraway stare.

How it rages like Hades in its requiem role,
while the chief fallen angel vies for one's soul.

With fiendish detest and repulsive disdain,
there's an odious hatred that thrives from one's pain.

Disdain for the living and contempt for the dead,
We dwell with the dragon in the Dungeon of Dread:

A demonic Necropolis without moral codes,
built to house pagans in these tortured abodes.

Possessed with the sullen, and somber with droll,
we search to escape this horrid Hell-hole.

Some call this a prison. Some say it's a jail.
Whatever the title, we are truly in Hell.

**THE JIG IS UP!**
By: Clint Cooper

Population growin', money flowin'
Cadillacs rollin', whores strollin'
Negotiations abandoned, whores stranded.
Crack use on the rise.
Infant mortality is no surprise.

Death and destruction run rampant throughout the land.
AIDS and crack killin' the Black man.
Gang violence at an all-time high.
Young men dying and don't know why.

The Governor claims it's all a lie.
The public wants justice; that's the cry.
The administration claims rehabilitation to the situation.
Public defender loses every litigation.

Penitentiaries built.
Warehouse 'em 'til they're all filled.
Society is scared to death.
Execute 'em 'til there are none left.

Sittin' here in my 6 x 6 cell
Reminiscing when all was well.
I see my life through the eyes of another.
The shame and grief that I brought to my mother

Why, my son, didn't you consider your ways?
These are my thoughts as I count the days.
Barbwire fences and iron gates,
My mind wonders about my fate.

I went to the Parole Board, seeking my release.
The question among them,
"Whose money will he decrease?"
I was turned down without a doubt.
We all know what that's about.

So, I will be out late.
My Caddie will be out-of-date.
My whores will no longer be strollin'.
In the graveyard, they'll be a rollin'.

Sixteen years later, I will be free.
Returnin' to the streets, but not as the same me.
Many have come and many have gone.
Some died and some went home.

**PRISON**
By: Darryl Payne

Prison is a place in people's minds
Many who don't know it are doing time:

Those who refuse to be all they can be
by stifling their ambitions, not letting their minds run free

Those who are afraid of a little work,
whose goals and dreams they tend to shirk

Those who let others lead them on,
who on life's chessboard are simple pawns

Those whose minds are slow as slugs,
hindered by the demons of alcohol and drugs

People who spread destruction everyday,
not realizing they destroy themselves that way

People who just can't seem to see
what it means to be really free.
For them, no bars are needed to hold
their minds which are stopped
Stone . . .Dead . . .Cold

I may have a number assigned to me
but my mind, heart and soul will always be free.
I refuse to let anyone hold me back
from achieving those things that I lack.
You see, no matter how much time I've been given,
**NOTHING WILL EVER HOLD ME IN PRISON!**

**OBLIVION**
By: Dennis E. Anderson

Oblivious to all things everywhere
The birds retreating to their nests at day's end
So seem the people out there
Snug retreats in havens of trees
Encompassing each other in solitude
Across the fence
Miles separated by wire and time
The gap widening our hapless homes
Vociferous din of colors and iron
Beat of gloves and bats punctuating, stop time
Another mark diminishing
The years to end a period
To a long sentence
Expletives bitterly drawn on
Day after day
Tired of the constant crying of others
Over and above sane thoughts
Desiring fences and time to pass the day
Retreating to havens of trees away
Oblivious to all things, everywhere

**I AM**

By: Herman M. Travis

I am a grain of sand in an hourglass.
I see from behind walls that I cannot escape.
But, such is the life that I lead.
Beautiful things surround me here everyday,
Yet, they do not exist in this world I occupy.
Each day that passes seems
no different than the day before.
The unsteady flow of others that may resemble
that which I am varies
with each elapse of granules.
We are all contained in this place of repetitiveness,
or for the lack of better wording,
"That which keeps repeating itself."
Forever seems such a long time to dwell
in a life such as this one.
One day I shall exist on a level of far greater horizons
than the one I currently reside in.
Then, I will become a grain of sand,
all those beautiful things I see . . .

## TIME

By: David W. Davis

Time has rushed by
in the blink of an eye,
'til to me it seems non-existent.
At first I cry,
then breathe deep and sigh.
How far shall I fall before time's spent?

## INCARCERATED

By: Maurice Coleman

This is the ultimate test,
for only a real man can stand alone
remain strong and
survive for the best.

This unexplainable experience
is detrimental psychologically and physically,
so it's a two-fold experience of pure Hell.
For a man will either bend like soft metals
or become hard like steel nails.
This is one place a strong man will find his true self
and a weak man will lose constantly,
until nothing is left.
This is truly a place of sorting out problems of all types.
A place to develop the patience and tolerance
and solitude necessary
to elevate your mind to supreme spiritual heights.
This pinnacle is truly where mental incarceration ends
and where life and psychological freedom begin.

## DOING TIME

By: Keith A. Luecke

You do your best in life; yet, sometimes you're wrong.
You end up in a place where you must struggle to be strong
You've already been through so much guilt, fear and humiliation
But no one ever cares here,
they just add more to your frustration.
Instead of building you up
and getting you back on your feet,
it seems their purpose is to constantly
grind you down in defeat.
"They" have a name,
it's the Department of Rehabilitation and Correction.
But they act more like
the Department of Hatred and Intimidation.
Most of those that are here
have committed a particular crime
They treat us as if we are not human
as we struggle to do our time.
We've made mistakes, and as such, it may be our fate,
but instead of rehabilitating us, they just make us all hate.

**REHABILITATION**
By: David W. Davis

If I am handicapped, who did it?

Welcome to the warehouse for
the storage of flesh and soul.
All of my daily choices
were wrenched from my control.
The value system is different, solely materialistic.
Knowing all I knew before, I would change, if only I could.
Reduced to a mere number and object upon their walls,
a notch upon their pistols, a place for their shit to fall
No desire to be a policeman, the president or the mayor.
No desiring human feelings or to even fucking care.

## THE CLUB WHERE THE MUSIC IS GONE

By: David W. Davis

Ours is a club quite exclusive.
And when you first enter in,
your mind shall require rearranging,
For it's like nowhere you've been,
For it's like nowhere you've been . . .

What we find amusing may shock you,
like the beatings, the pain and the boys.
We value quite high those who fluently lie,
and your fear is a source of great joy.

At first, you may drift off to sleep,
when you think you've figured things clear,
until the screams late at night, the pleading in fright
Awaken! For the reaper is near!

In our club pure love's been perverted,
abused and confused for so long.
Live here and you'll soon be converted,
To the club where the music is gone,
To the club where the music is gone . . .

**TIME FOR TIME**
By: Robert L. Hevlin Jr.

A never-ending process is the crucible of time.
Progressing to a finite end, a paradox of time.
A never ceasing constant and a prodigy to me;
Though just a child yesterday, how does that seem to be?
And now that I am older, it accelerates its climb.
though when I was a younger man,
a day seemed trapped in time.
No matter how it seems to be, the hour's growing late.
For in the end, we all will find, we all must meet our fate.
We're held within its vacuum, but in the end you'll see,
It's just another state of mind.
Our thoughts will hold the key.
And yes, the clock is ticking, but now it's on my side,
For I've mastered my contrivance,
and I now have time to bide.
Though I've aged upon reflection,
while I've sat to write this rhyme,
That's just another retrospect of living life with time.

**MY TIME**

By: James C. Johnson Jr.

Each tic of the clock
I grow older by the second.
Minutes turn into hours . . .
Hours turn into months . . .
Months turn into years . . .
Years turn into . . . my tears.

**TOTAL ECLIPSE**
By: James C. Johnson Jr.

Blinded by darkness,
Shades of night,
Useless vision,
Touching is life.
Senses intrepidly guide the way.
Incandescence is but a dream.
Braille is the key to the universe.

## REALITY'S HALLUCINATIONS

By: Edward Armstrong

Do you see what I see?
The vanity of man now a fatal disease.
They run and they laugh.
They mock and they kill.
Condemning all those born of a different will.
Freedom granted to some, refused to others,
while society turns to insanity like a child to its mother.
Sickness considered health while health becomes a myth.
Choices carry judgment; silence begets gifts.
A world I did not choose, yet now seek to escape.
Foreign to their acceptance, never once embraced.
I want to love them as they refuse to love me.
My fate becomes loneliness. My tears become seas.
Imprisoned and born of a different will.
My flesh is not enough, my dreams too, they wish to kill.

## LAWS OF THE JUNGLE

By: Joshua Aaron Wiltfong

It's not easy being locked up.
Your heart's filled with grief about to erupt.

The strong will always prey on the weak.
There are certain challenges you have to beat.

I try everyday to grow even stronger,
Hoping and praying I'll survive a little longer.

I don't want to be here; my world has crumbled.
But I've learned to live by . . .the laws of the jungle.

## ONLY IN PRISON

By: Raven Everett

Yesterday I remember sitting here thinking.
Now, here I am sitting here today, thinking about what I thought about yesterday. And I can't help but wonder what my thoughts will be tomorrow because . . .
My thoughts seem to be the same day after day . . .
Year after year . . .
month after month . . .
week after week . . .
every hour . . .
every minute . . .
and every second.

Now tell me, what type of environment can cause so much confusion in a human being's life?
ONLY IN PRISON---

How many places can you go in this world and find a grown man crying?
How many times have you seen green eggs, green hot dogs and burgundy bologna?
I thought this type of stuff was only in books.
Where can you go and see people getting jumped on for no reason at all?
ONLY IN PRISON---

Have you ever seen someone that was on top? Out there balling out of control, driving big cars, owning big houses and partying all the time. I'm talking about the type of person who thought the world was his. Now, he doesn't have seventy-eight cents to buy a bag of chips. How many thugs do you know are out like that?
ONLY IN PRISON---

How many thugs do you know that are scared to take showers?
How many places do you know where they serve more than one God?
Do you remember that school bully named "Jack"?
Yeah, but it ain't "Jack" anymore, it's "Jackie."
How did that happen?
ONLY IN PRISON---

Did you see that dude stab what's-his-name sixteen times with that shank?
I did.
Did you know they made places were a grown man can't use the restroom in peace and scared to go to sleep at night? It does happen. Where?
ONLY IN PRISON

## THOUGHTS OF A CONVICT

By: Perry L. Rickman

Someday the gates will open
and once again I'll be free
A thought that makes me wonder,
what will soon become of me?

Have I a better future out there awaiting me?
Not like the one that I'd once known
Will I be accepted by society?
Or will I be forced to walk alone?

Is there even an opportunity for a job
for an ex-convict such as I?
Or will I be forced to sell drugs again
in order to live and get by?

What about the friends that I once knew
but haven't seen in many years?
Will they really accept my friendship,
without the doubts and fears?

What is there awaiting me
outside these prison gates?
Is there another chance to be free
or is it now just too damn late?

**THESE WALLS**
By: Allen Gentry

If these walls could speak, they would tell a million stories,
but they choose to stay silent 'cause they know no glory.
I can count the cracks like so many years I've wasted.
So many victories almost won I could just about taste it.
It's hard to have faith, looking through my eyes,
Been sold too many dreams and told too many lies.
They confine my physical being yet my spirit wants to run,
My talent put down on paper flows freely from my tongue.
Of course, I want success, who in their right mind don't,
Sure, I'm gonna do dirt for it,
who in their right mind won't.
'Cause I choose to utilize the tools in my environment.
It ain't always my fault when shit ends up in confinement.
Without expression there's no action,
if we can't speak, then we stay weak.
I refuse to lie down and die or humble at your feet
The institution of democracy bleeds life to anarchy
I've been silent long enough, tired of hypocrisy
I've got to speak out, 'cause it's my seed that's next in line
And I'd die before I let him suffer a fate worse than mine
Corruption at the highest levels but
Mr. Man don't pay the price
Instead it falls on the heads of minorities
filling their lives with strife
I got dreams, but it don't seem like I'm getting any closer
Why is it that my nightmares seem like
there're becoming worser?
Clear my mind, 'cause it's cluttered
with so much chaos and confusion
No wonder I stay high, it helps me see through the illusion,
of better days and better ways with no ending conclusion.
Though I try to stay levelheaded in
whatever path I'm choosing.
For my wife and young J. D., I'd put it all on the line
Carry the world on my shoulders
and stop the hands of time.
It's the real deal for me 'cause I'm living in the trencher.
If I was meant to be weak, I'd be scared and defenseless.

But I'm strong 'cause you are testing me
And I'm wrong, but you are blessing me.
Bound to get it right eventually, if it is the death of me
Look for direction in a higher power, searching for a sign,
Hoping I come across one to help deal with the hard times.
But being honest lately, it feels like a goose chase.
Keep ending up where I started, beginning to lose face.
They tell me faith can move mountains,
but I'm having trouble with these walls.
I accept it 'cause I have to maintain through it all
For this, I thank my momma,
'cause through her I learned strength
Her examples of pulling through
and making do at any length.
I live with the pain, 'cause pain lets me know I'm still here.
I contain my anger, 'cause it overcomes my fear.
My destiny isn't clear to me; it seems all out of focus.
I guess if I talked loud enough,
then no one would take notice.
I can still see that kid in the mirror
I know from back in the day.
Now I see reflections of my son in many of the same ways.
I'll break my neck to keep him from falling where I fell.
'Cause I be damn if he gonna hear,
what these walls got to tell.

## REFLECTIONS

By: Joseph Modica

Things are slow here right now. There's no reason to hurry for I'm stuck in a place where time has no relevance. While I walk to "chow," everyone around me is restless and trying to get their first servings like spiders that have just caught an insect in their web. The spider wraps the victim quickly and effectively, not wasting a second lest her new meal escape. The same is true for my co-offenders, as soon as they get their trays, the food is gone with such speed that it makes you wonder if their taste buds even registered it before it was in their bellies. Just as well, though, for the food here isn't much to write home about, quite bland, if you know what I mean. Then off again, quickly depositing their empty trays into a little square in the wall where they magically disappear.

I look up at the blue sky and the clouds above. I wonder if anyone else is looking at those same clouds and if so, what are they thinking about. Do they think about their freedom? Do they think that the glare of the sun that makes them purple is as beautiful as I think it is? Do they notice how the moon looks like a giant marble, or that it is barely a sliver, depending on what time of month it is? Do they say, "Oh, there's the North Star, so bright in the sky!" and then realize that it's in the southern sky? Maybe they notice a planet such as Mars or Venus in the dusk.

I look down at the grass and notice the color that means so much to me, green. It makes me think of life, but at the same time, there's brown grass next to it. Death can be so close and we don't even notice it. I say to myself, "I take so much for granted. I never know when I might lose a loved one. This is no place to be for that to happen." I then notice the cement that's below me, how it's all cracked up and worn out, how it has separated from itself. It reminds me of my relationships with the ones I care about. I step all over them so much that they are worn out from dealing with me so they separate themselves from me and keep moving further from me. I guess it's really me, me moving further away for I push their help away.

As I move on, I notice the guards and wonder, if I can grin hello and smile, will they do the same? Most of them don't though. I think it's a fear of getting too close to the inmates. I do this with everyone. I make eye contact even with other offenders. Usually not with a smile though, just with a nod of the head that says, "What's up?"

As I sit down to eat, I try to stay unbiased about the food in front of me, well, at least until I say grace. You see, it usually doesn't look that good, let alone taste that good. After grace, though, it seems to receive a miracle, the miracle of taste. I eat it gratefully. Of course, the salt and pepper on the table does help.

As I slowly walk back to my humble cell, I admire the sky and the ground once more. As I begin to smoke a cigarette, that always seems to taste so good after a meal, I wonder about my existence once again. I say this because lately I seem to question why I'm here on Earth, here in Missouri, here in prison. Is there some hidden agenda that I haven't found yet? Was I placed in prison for more reasons than committing a crime? I don't know, but constantly I question.

I slowly inhale my cigarette one last time for the taste doesn't seem so great anymore, even though I've only smoked half of it. I venture over to my little window to look out at an existence beyond the walls and fences that keep such a menace to society out of sight and mind of the *good* people of the world. I can see the tops of some big trees, probably ones that block wind and create shade for some farmhouse. There's also a large power line that flows by giving light and warmth to free individuals close by to power their TV's, microwaves and garage door openers. There are birds sitting on the wire, some bunched up close to one another, maybe trying to keep warm. There are some alone, not part of the group. Poor birds, they have no one to chirp to. There is no one to hear them sing their song. I feel like those birds, so close to the others, but away in their own world, feeling that no one can understand them.

I slowly retire to my bed and look around the room, staring at the wall outlet, then noticing some dried up toothpaste on the wall that someone in the past used to hang something up. It's now as solid as the grout that holds the bricks together, the same bricks that surround my room to keep me where I belong.

I can tell depression is settings in. I have no desire to do anything. I just want to lie around and sleep. I know I should work out and work off my love handles and tighten my stomach. I know if I read, it will better my spelling and kill time, but I just don't feel like it. I tell myself that when I get to a more permanent camp, I will start all of this. I won't be locked down so much and will want to do more, that all of this lockdown is causing these feelings. Somewhat true, but I'm lazy. For the most part, laziness never gets one anywhere. That's probably why I like to be instantly gratified, "No work necessary!" I just don't know. It's hard to keep your hopes up in such an environment.

## MIRROR OF CONFUSION

By: Edward Armstrong

There is something staring at me,
yet I don't know what it is.
Its eyes are dark and cold and as deep as an abyss.
Its voice is unheard, but I can feel its pain.
As the tears run down its face like that of newborn rain,
it hides from the light, for darkness is its friend.
A prisoner of its own world, a life sentence it shall serve,
a sentence of sorrow and loneliness
that no one truly deserves.
There's something familiar about its face.
I've seen it somewhere before.
Ah, perhaps it's the fiend of my nightmares
coming once again to wage war.
Perhaps it's the face of the child that I see
so often in my dreams,
the child who fears all that which is unknown and unseen.
It is just then that I am frightened,
for this face speaks to me,
"What are you staring at fool?
Do you not recognize what you see?
You feed me your fears in this mirror of confusion."
It was just then that I recognized
what I thought could never be;
the fiend of my nightmares,
***that fiend was me***.

# LIFE CHOICES

## JUNKIE

By: Steven Wittman

**Tap, tap, tap**
the needle into the vein,
*P-u-l-l* – blood mixes
with a solution of relief.

All women are the same,
Gone for three days,
Clothes gone, money too . . .
All she left was a note.

Parents fight,
All day and all night,
Black eyes, bruises…
Xmas presents are few.

Rent past due,
Does the phone work?
Bills filed away
. . . in the trash.

Who's knocking
on the door?
Bondsman, probation officer?
Connection I owe?

**Tap, tap, tap**
the needle into the vein,
*P-u-s-h . . .p-u-l-l . . .*
Reliable relief.

**THE ROAD I'VE PAVED**
By: Larry Cherry

I don't know why I
do some of the things I do.
The mind is a complex thing, they say,
and it seems to be true.

I can't embrace the future,
because I'm still living in the past.
Why can't I get my life straightened out,
is a question often asked?

To that I have no answer, but sometimes I get a clue,
And then it's gone again like something I never knew.

Why, I ask myself, do I put myself
through all of this pain?
With most of the choices I've made in life,
pain is all I've gained.

I'm stuck in a vicious cycle that seems a lot like fate.
What is my breaking point? How much more can I take?

My mind's pushed over the edge
by choices I've already made.
My descent into an eternal HELL assured by
the road I've already paved.

**CRACKED UP**

By: Asa G. A. Collins

In the haze of yonder dreams gone wild,
she walks stealthily and sure.
Jittering nerves are calmed in her presence.
Beckoning a master to rule heaven's fallen star.
And Hate told me there are no white gods.

Foolish whims become the cornerstones of an empire.
A fire's rage, the light of the world.
Fire on one end,
a fool on the other
And Hate told me there are no white gods.

She dances before me in flames,
yet, I am the slave at her whip
Tantalized are her jagged curves
made smooth to flow like cream.
And Hate told me there are no white gods.

With pious lips I inhale her mist
choking on her laughter inside of me.
Her screwing me,
choking on but one of many good love thangs.
And Hate told me there are no white gods.

In wrenching pain,
on penitent knees,
Bowed reverently before ivory stones
And Hate told me there are no white gods.

**COURAGE**
By: Paul T. Crowl, Jr.

I've dreamed many dreams that never came true
I've seen them vanish at dawn,
But I've realized enough of my dreams,
thank God, to make me want to dream on.

I've prayed many prayers when no answer came,
though I waited patiently and long,
But answers have come to enough prayers
to make me keep praying on.

I've trusted many a friend that failed me,
and left me to weep, alone.
But I've found enough of my friends true-blue,
to make me keep trusting on.

I've sown many seed that fell by the way
for the birds to feed upon.
But I've held enough golden sheaves in my hands
to make me keep sowing on.

I've drained the cup of disappointment and pain
and gone many days without song.
But I've sipped enough nectar from the roses of life
to make me want to live on.

**REALITY**

By: Michael Vineyard

In another world, away from the sun
With room to play, but not to run
Watching the days turn into years
I'm hiding behind a wall of fears.

But nothing really matters at all.
Reality is bars and a forty-foot wall
where pain and violence are all I see
of society's attempt to rehabilitate me.

Lost in this fantasy, all alone
trying survival on my own.
I close my eyes to dream of bliss
but all my dreams end like this:

In an ivory tower of virgin white
I'm sitting alone trying to write
while some maniac I'll never meet
plays with a gun on a wall of concrete.

## IMAGINATION

By: Duane Anthony Brown

As we all know, the definition of "imagination," as per Webster's dictionary is:

> The power of the mind to form a mental image or concept of something that is unreal or not present.

Have you ever wondered why some of us have very active imaginations, while in the same context, this concept is virtually non-existent to others? I've had the opportunity over the years to ponder this enigma and I've arrived at some quite fascinating conclusions. Allow me to explain . . .

I've learned that if a person has an extremely powerful imagination, he or she can describe a place, an act or even an item to the point that they allow others to see it, feel it or even experience it. You see, if a person is articulate enough, as well as descriptive enough, that individual can create a vivid clarity that is almost real for the reader or audience.

Before I continue, let's try a little experiment, shall we? I'm going to depict a warm, summer day. Close your eyes and picture this scene:

You're walking along a beach with your mate. The sea gulls are singing their melodic tunes, and gliding on the warm currents of air that seem to come from the very sand that you're walking barefoot on. Off to your right, the ocean waves are crashing on the beach and going back out with an almost hypnotic motion . . .

With each breeze you feel a light, almost gentle caress of salt spray, as it touches your skin. As you walk along holding hands with your mate, your nose catches the subtle, but unmistakable scent of coconuts as the other "sun-worshipers" who share your space, apply tanning lotion to their bodies in slow, sensual strokes . . .

Now, those of you who took my little test, and have active imaginations, would not have ended where I did. Six out of ten of you would have continued with the vision and created your own ending, which I believe, would have been an intimate encounter with your mate in some secluded spot on that beach.

The key is this: by inserting little trigger words like *hypnotic motion*, *gentle caress*, and *slow, sensual, strokes* into my story, I led the reader to think of it as an intimate encounter. The reality here is this: anyone can develop an imagination . . . as long as you have someone who can plant a suggestion in your mind, all that's left to do is concentrate and let your mind do the rest. Isn't the human mind a wonderful device?

## PLIGHT
By: Sharpe Clayton

Where I come from has no bearing on my plight.
No one can actually say what is behind some closed doors.
I can only open them to master my own fears.
Bad experiences happen sometimes, and I have survived.
Therefore, I must carry on.
Cries are only cries if
I dwell in a world seeking compassion.
Life owes me nothing!
So I must continue to dream, plan and act on all my issues,
to place success in the palm of my hands,
because nothing comes to a dreamer but a dream.
I sit and meditate in my moment of glory,
being all I can be simply because
I will let nothing polish the essence of me.

**ON A MOUNTAIN**

By: Daniel Mullins

One day I climbed a mountain. It was an early morning in August, "Dog Days." I don't really know what possessed me to start out that day. It was a typically beautiful Appalachian morning. The mist was low in the valleys with only the uppermost peaks of the mountains showing through. I had just awakened and stepped outside on the front porch with my morning coffee in hand. It was a bad time for me. I had recently separated from my wife and I was missing my two-year-old son.

I gazed up at the mountain, finished my coffee and started walking up the foothills. Along the way, about a quarter of a mile up, I came upon a small isolated cemetery. Up to this point, the area was heavily wooded, and I had been following what appeared to be a deer trail. The cemetery was in a clearing; a small square cut out of the forest. One grave, in particular, appeared well attended. I noticed a piece of paper lying under a small stone near the headstone. Feeling a little guilty, I picked up the piece of paper and gazed at the childlike handwriting therein. It was a letter from a little boy, apparently addressed to his father whose grave I was standing over. The letter made me think of my own son, whom I hadn't seen in several months. The cemetery was for mountain folk, who would carry their beloved up the side in order to bury them on the mountain. I placed the boy's letter back under the stone, cleared some leaves away from the grave and continued on my way.

The sun began to show through the mist the higher I climbed. As noted, it was "Dog Days" and there had been warnings issued directing folks to stay out of the mountains. The hot weather had a strange effect on the animals, especially snakes, which tended to be more aggressive than usual. Conscious of this, I searched for and found a suitable forked hickory stick.

The climb was growing steeper and I was getting thirsty. I had not thought to bring any water along, my morning coffee having worn off an hour earlier. Up ahead, I could see some rock formations from some ancient glacial movement. Off to my left, perhaps fifty yards away, I could see the furtive movements of a small pack of wild dogs. I had seen them earlier. They seemed to be following me up the mountain.

As I neared the top of the mountain, the craggy rock formations towered above me. I had no climbing equipment, and I hadn't told anyone that I was going climbing. I was worried. If I had an unfortunate run-in with an irritable den of Copperheads, or fell from the rocks, it would be all over. I started to turn around and go back down the mountain, but stopped. It occurred to me that I'd been doing things half-assed all my life. I asked myself why had I started out on this hike. The answer was clear and simple, to get to the top of the mountain. My thirst, and the fear of dying up there just about sapped my spirit. Still, something would not let me give up. I put down the hickory stick and grabbed hold of the lowest boulder. Pulling myself up, I continued to climb, conscious of every crack and crevice in the rocks. My throat was dry and my breath was coming in gasps.

While climbing I made noise, so as not to surprise any unsuspecting snakes. At one point, about twenty feet away, I saw a big Copperhead cooling itself on a ledge. I continued to climb. Near the top, the rocks were stacked up like steps leading to the uppermost boulder. I walked up and gazed around me. The sight was undoubtedly the most beautiful thing that I have ever seen. Stretched out before me was the Appalachian Mountain Range. The remaining morning mists were lying like a blanket in the valleys. I felt on top of the world, the mountains seemed to speak to me, congratulating me on my quest. It was the most spiritual moment of my life.

Eventually, I made my way back down the mountain. I passed through the little cemetery and said goodbye to my curious canine climbing companions. Back on flat land, things were a little anxious. My recent girlfriend was worried, and she had a park ranger with her. I received a well-meaning lecture about tromping off unannounced into the mountains alone.

Looking back on that day, I can see how the experience has affected my life. Every obstacle in my path is measured against that day on the mountain. My run-ins with ruthless and corrupt people, the locked doors and adverse opinions are likened to the rocks and snakes. Conversely, my friends, love and hope are likened to the curious wild dogs, the small cemetery, and the little boy's letter to his father.

At some point in our lives, if we are fortunate, we will experience some event that transcends everything that has happened before in our life. This was mine. It has taken the better part of a lifetime to find my true spirit. But I found it one day on a mountain.

**A GREATER PURPOSE**

By: Joe Trevino

From days of old
my life unfolds.
Tears, like rain, I've cried.
My mother left.
My father's gone.
Alone, I wondered why.
From youth I prayed
my sword one day
might valiantly defend,
a child's life
in guiding strength
from love a heart can mend.
A warrior now
sworn to uphold
the truth in life I see.
Strategic plan:
achieve your goals
Your life is love for me.
Find happiness and do your best.
Be good to those you know.
Trust your heart. Dare to dream.
We'll make our vision grow.

**PUNISHMENT**
By: Jason M. Naylor

It's time to sing my last song in tune
for who knows what tomorrow will bring
Time fades away.
I've surely paid.
I know I'm wrong.
Please forgive me
and release the pain.

Let's go, son.
It's time for your PUNISHMENT
for who knows how long.
Time fades away.
I've surely paid.
I don't know what else to say
But please, pray for me.
It's the only thing that turns
us around.

It's all said and done.
Fate's wound down for me.
Don't do the same!
Promise Me!
YOU WON'T DO THE SAME!

**WOVEN TALES**

By: A. Broomfield

A fibrous beginning
inside the heart
of tales woven
creating a life of their own.
Seed's own
planted in life's past
Designs of destiny's path
await fate's intervention
to unlock the doors
that he now stands before
Behind these are the secrets of life,
the awakening of consciousness
from the purity one finds
in the realization of one's true self.

## SO MANY CHANGES

By: Keith A. Luecke

Life has so many changes.
We need to look and see,
our effect upon each other
in our struggle to be free.
Our lives can touch so many
that we don't even consider.
We should try to remember
that we're all in this together.

Tell those that are around you
how much you truly care,
for there's no guarantee of tomorrow
that you'll be able to share
the feelings that you carry
and the love you wish to give.
For if there's no tomorrow
how much harder it is to live
knowing you loved somebody
and didn't get a chance to say,
how much they truly meant to you
before they were taken away

Life has so many changes.
Don't let them pass by.
Share your love with others
before you must say goodbye.

## SAYING

By: Steven York Lent

Sometimes our greatest discoveries
are found with our eyes closed . . .
At times, they are never opened wide enough.

**CHASING THE THUNDER**
By: Steven J. Anderson

Lightning streaks through a darkened sky,
A distant look in the old man's eye
The rolling boom of the distant thunder,
He feels the hurt that's deep down under.

Wind blowing softly, the smell of spring,
Clouds drifting slowly as the birds all sing.
Lifting his head to the rising sun,
It's time once more; it's time to run.

Chasing the thunder from hill to hill,
He'll chase the thunder 'til time stands still.
He can't look back at memories that be,
He'll chase the thunder from sea to sea.

From childhood to manhood only he could hear,
A far distant calling; an irrational fear
Never stayed put, no root to grow,
A hunger and push only he does know.

Women he met passed like seasons,
His love for them had no rhyme or reason.
Holding them close throughout the night,
Telling goodbyes with the morning light.

He'd traveled to lands so distant and far,
Wandering around lost like a falling star.
Roads always seemed to lead to one place,
He'd trudge through life, a smile on his face.

At times he stopped for a breath or two,
Thought maybe he'd stay, but he always knew,
Over that hill where his eyes couldn't see,
Is where he would go, where he would be.

Chasing the thunder from hill to hill,
He'll chase the thunder 'til time stands still.
He can't look back at memories that be,
He'll chase the thunder from sea to sea.

The older he got, the past held tight,
Things he'd done wrong, but at the time felt right.
Behind him all bridges, burnt to the ground,
No memories of him for he wasn't around.

The people who cared thought he noticed them not,
The people he loved, he loved them a lot.
Seemed that he was indifferent, that he paid no mind,
But his heart was broken when he left them behind.

Finally, he found the love of his life,
He fought the past to make her his wife.
He fought with passion to clear his name,
But a wandering gypsy, forever his fame

As a husband, she took him for her love was great,
She'd ease his pains; she was his soul mate.
They held in their hands each other's heart,
Meant for each other from the very start.

Their children and grandchildren brought out their smiles,
Finally, he knew it was worth all of the miles.
The traveling, the running, never stopping at all,
His hunting was over. He'd found his heart's call.

Hands holding tightly, he looked into her eyes,
He told of his love, how it would never die.
Though one of us may live, when the other is gone,
Our love is as certain as the morning dawn.

As all things do, time caught up with them,
He couldn't understand why, it was her not him.
Wiping the tears with the back of his hand,
He gazed at the roses that covered their land.

She’d told him one night, so long ago,
There’s something my dear, I want you to know.
If something ever happens and I’m gone before you,
I’ll be with you always for my love is that true.

With that thought in his heart, his face to the sun,
The old man smiled, for again he must run.
Though this time around, alone he’d not be,
So he’d chase the thunder to the shining sea.

Chasing the thunder from hill to hill,
He’ll chase the thunder ‘til time stands still.
He can’t look back at memories that be,
He’ll chase the thunder from sea to sea.

## CIRCLES

By: Richard Horton

I sit alone in my cell of white, the world outside still turns.
The Blues, a constant reminder of the freedom for which I yearn.

Once again, I've played the fool; sitting and thinking is all I do.
Once again, I let my wants rule, when I should've been holding you.

I have no one else to blame for the situation that I'm in.
I know this road by name. It's someplace I've already been.

Why do I do these things? Why am I so irate?
Why, when everything gets better, it's always a little too late?

One of these lonely days or nights, I just might figure it out.
I'll stop all these pointless fights, that's when I'll win the 'bout.

Until that day comes along, I'll have to sit and ponder.
For within these four walls, I have plenty of time to wonder.

I still long for the day when I'll be free to roam.
Oh, what a beautiful day that'll be, when I'll finally be going home.

What will I find that day? What mysteries do wait?
What'll be on the other side when they decide to open that gate?

I hope for a love that'll never end, a love of give and take.
One that's strong enough to bend, but never will break.

I must keep looking out there, searching, for my true love.
She's gotta be out there somewhere, the woman I'm dreaming of.

## ADAM'S DILEMMA

By: Joseph M. Myers

Adam awoke and felt the tingle of a message from the Witches' Council tapping at his skull. He slowly sat up in bed and allowed the message to play in his mind. It was as he feared. With a magical wave of his fingers he turned on the night lamp. He tenderly looked over the still, sleeping figure of Sardonica beside him. Her full name was Sardonica Maori Fura Destonia and she was an alien. Oh, she was basically humanoid, but what an exotic beautiful humanoid she was. She had long silky ebony hair. Her skin was smooth and covered in short fine ebony hair that gave her elegant, segmented body a glossy appearance. She had two nodules on each side of her abdomen, her limbs were multi-jointed and her multifaceted eyes were a deep amber color. Her race was called the Lamorta and they were dying off.

She had been sent as an emissary of her people to Earth to seek help. The Witches' Council had managed to divert her craft from landing and explained to her that mortal humans were still very xenophobic and not ready for encounters of the extraterrestrial kind. Her need and charisma persuaded the council to provide her with a guide to allow her to get to know the people of Earth without risk to her personal well-being.

That is how Adam came to know and love her. He had been chosen to be her guide because of the simple fact that he was half human on his father's side. His older sister was too busy teaching and Adam was in between music gigs and hadn't been seeking any work as an illustrator. When Adam first met Sardonica, it was a simple matter to put a minor glamour on her to make her appear to others less than her seven-foot-six self.

She had been utterly fascinated by human architecture, "It's so vertical and horizontal!" she had exclaimed.

He had wondered what type of help her people needed. The answer surprised him.

"We need mating partners." She smiled at his stunned expression. Her face became grim as she continued, "Our men are dying off faster than we reproduce. Our scientists are very sure that our DNA is compatible with other species so that we may procreate with others and keep our race from dying off."

That was the beginning of a fantastic romance that was worlds beyond anything Adam had ever experienced. Her people also had the custom of marriage and that is exactly what Adam had in mind for the both of them.

To his dismay, the Witches' Council was utterly against their plans for marriage. Adam was furious. He pointed out the marriage of his own mother and father and the happiness they shared despite the interference of overbearing witch relatives. He was shocked to hear his own sister siding with the Witches' Council.

"We don't know enough about her people," was her response.

Now he had the Witches' Council's final decision. Adam had been given two choices. It was time to inform Sardonica what had happened. Oh, the Witches' Council was blind! So what if she could leap tall buildings in a single bound? So what if she could do some incredibly kinky things while hanging from the ceiling? This last thought brought a smile to his face as he gently awoke his dear love.

"Oh Adam, I have such wonderful news, I am pregnant with your children. In a few months of your time you'll be a very proud father."

"Sardonica, that's wonderful, but I have bad news. The Witches' Council has ruled that if we continue our plans to marry they will strip me of my witchcraft. Since I've already made it plain to them I'll not change my mind, they are allowing me to perform a few final acts of magic before my powers are gone forever." He waved his hands and she watched in fascination as their few meager possessions packed themselves into suitcases that had appeared out of thin air.

"And now for our final destination." He gestured as if gathering their belongings and throwing them. The next thing Sardonica knew she was sitting on a tree stump on her home world with her spacecraft only a few feet away and Adam standing in front of her.

"I can feel my magic starting to slip away so I must cast my final spell." The air grew still as he begin to speak:

"With honeyed breath and beestings,
With feather down as spiders sing,
Allow this warlock's form to rearrange,
To become as my love's form and Council's order bids me change.
So change, change,
Oh, rearrange this warlock's form to be,
Change to something more suitable by my heart's decree!"

A symphony of light and music cascaded around Adam's body as Sardonica watched in dreadful fear.

Adam felt his joints break and shatter, then alter to a multi-jointed formation. His eyesight grew hazy as his pupils multiplied tenfold, then grew intensely sharp as he realized he could count each individual hair that was sprouting along his body. The final change came as Adam's body shrank from six-foot-two to three-foot-four.

"RUN, ADAM, RUN!" Sardonica screamed as he gripped a nearby tree as if to restrain himself.

Adam could only watch as four extra limbs sprouted from the nodules at her side and her multifaceted eyes changed from amber to glowing red.

"Oh, Adam!" she shrieked as she bounded over to him and grasped him in her multiple appendages, "I wish you hadn't cast that last spell. Now I can no longer resist, but I must tell you why. The females of my species have an unusual biological urge to consume our mates after we have mated. That is why our species is dying off. If only you had remained human, my biological urges wouldn't be overpowering my reasoning or my love. Oh, Adam, forgive me!"

His last sight of her strangely wasn't her mouth distorted and enlarged by the ring of fangs that had sprouted there, but of the red hourglass shape that was normal part of her abdomen. Then he saw nothing more.

Adam awoke, fear drenching his body in heavy beads of sweat. Sardonica slept still, but tears ran down her face as she moaned in horror at what she believed herself to be doing.

Standing at the front of the bed was Adam's sister. She smiled at him then looked with pity at Sardonica's tear-stained face.

"You can wake her in a moment," she said to Adam, "The Witches' Council ruled that you marry her, but you must never sacrifice your magic for her and obviously, you must never transform into a male of her species. Her love for you is strong and almost tore the dream-spell to shreds that you unknowingly shared with her. She almost resisted her natural biological urge for you. Be grateful Adam. Most of her species wouldn't have hesitated. Oh, and if I were you, I'd get a bigger place. Her people are egg-layers and one pregnancy usually means hundreds of children." Adam stared in horror at Sardonica's slightly swollen belly as images of diaper bills floated in front of his eyes.

## CHOICES

By: Joshua Aaron Wiltfong

Is this a dream?
Or is it real?
I've been through so much,
I can't even feel.

I just want to break down,
but I can't shed a tear.
I'm in no position to cry
and no position to fear.

I'm surrounded by people,
and at the same time, alone.
I wish I could just open my eyes
and be standing at home.

Everyone says they know
but they really don't.
They say they will,
but I say I won't.

Everywhere I turn
they say that God is the key.
But if they knew what I've been through
then my view, they would see.

## THE PURCHASE

By: Donald E. Tennyson

As soon as she opened the box, she knew this one was different. For one thing, it was larger than the last one she had purchased. This one looked a lot sturdier which was very important to a woman like her. She took it out of the box. It was hard where it needed to be yet flexible in other places. "Yes!" she exclaimed, "this one should fit nicely."

She held it in her hands, turning it around so that she could see it from different angles. Then she gently caressed her face with it. It felt nice next to her skin. She couldn't wait to try it out, remembering the last one she got. She should have tried out the others before she purchased this one, she thought. However, these things are personal. They have to be handled delicately and in private. Sure, they have places where a girl could try things like this out in relative privacy, but that was too much work. You never really know who may be watching. You hear about things like that all the time, some pervert sneaking around with some small video camera tucked in some out-of the-way place on his body recording unsuspecting women in private, compromising moments.

"That's all I need," she thought, "to see myself on some adult website." What would her co-workers think? It was bad enough that she had to resort to things like this. Sure, she was getting along in age and she hadn't had a real date in . . .well, a long time, but she had class and style. That's why she had bought this "damn thing" in the first place! She told herself she knew what she needed and what's wrong with having a little fun now and then?

She looked at the clock on the mantle, 7:30. If she left at 8:30 she could get there by nine. She had a whole hour to shower and get ready. That was more than enough time to try this thing out.

She took her new purchase upstairs to her bedroom and lay on her bed. She got undressed. She stood there looking at herself in her vanity mirror, "Gosh! Has it been that long?" she asked herself.

She fought the desire to try "it" at work in the mirror to see what "it" would do for her body; but she had been working all day and she really needed to shower first. She did have some dignity even if she did have to resort to buying this thing.

She turned the shower on. It was warm. As soon as she stepped in, she wished she had taken the time to run herself a bath. "Yes, a bath would be so nice right now," she thought; but that would take longer and she wanted to spend as much time trying "it" out as possible. She finished showering and toweled dry.

As she sat in front of the mirror drying her hair and counting the lines in a face that was handsome (which was the politically correct way of saying old) she reflected on a life spent being "good." She worked hard for everything she had and she didn't ask for anything she didn't earn. But when she felt she had earned it, she demanded and expected it. She lived her life by this motto: you don't have to respect me; just don't disrespect me.

She had been working for almost twenty-three years. She worked her way up from receptionist, to office manager, to District Vice-President with very little patience for distractions. She realized this was the reason she was alone. There had been men in her life, but it seemed sooner or later her career would get in the way and she would wind up having to choose.

She finished drying her hair, brushed it and put it up into a bun. She stood and took a long look at herself in the mirror. For a fifty-year-old, she had to admit, she still had a nice shape. Sure her hips were a little wider, her shoulders weren't as straight, and maybe her butt sagged just a bit, but she had grace. She carried herself well. She had caught the men around the office staring at her ass more than once. She could still turn a head or two.

"So why do I need this damn thing laying on my bed?" she thought.

She remembered what the first one felt like. It was uncomfortable and embarrassing to think she had to resort to this device. She had almost given up, but she talked herself into giving it one more try. The first one was too small, or maybe she was too rough with it, she didn't know. But this one looked good.

She walked over to her bed. It was lying there like all those years she had lived: lifeless and dull, yet filled with promise and hope. Maybe this simple device was the answer. Maybe its use was what she needed to get that last chance she so desperately wanted.

She sat next to "it" feeling very vulnerable suddenly. Like, somehow her future depended on how this simple, man-made device fit. This was troubling to her because it went straight to the heart of who she believed she was. She was strong, independent and most of all, proud. Proud of who she was and all she had accomplished. So why was her life all of a sudden, dependent on some external thing to help her feel worthy and admirable.

"I should get rid of this thing right now!" she thought. But as she sat, nude, feeling insufficiently defended by all of her life's accomplishments, she allowed herself to be persuaded by the temptation of this thing. She reached with reluctant hands and picked it up.

She relaxed, or tried to. She knew that it would be easier if she were calm. Still sitting, she faced the mirror. She had to see herself. She took a deep breath, held it for a moment, and slowly exhaled, letting all of her reluctance, guilt and shame, out with her breath.

It was time. She placed the device under her sagging breasts, and while holding it there with her left hand; she pulled the straps with her right. "Wow!" she thought, "that's tight!" It was also uncomfortable.

She stood. That was better. Standing took some of the pressure off. She placed the straps over her shoulders, wiggled a bit, and noticed the difference. This one was very different from the other one. It felt much better. She felt much better. She admired herself standing there nude, in front of the mirror. Her stomach was pretty flat, her legs were shaped. She was all-woman. Seeing herself nude, modeling in her bedroom, made her feel young and alive and sexy.

She put her hands on her hips. She turned to the left then to the right. "Yes," she thought, "I like this one."

She started to feel a little foolish for making such big deal out of this thing. Maybe it was the fact that in less than an hour she would be surrounded by many of her friends and colleagues, being honored for her many years of accomplishments and vital commitment to her job.

"Still," she thought, "it's just a push-up bra!"

## KNOW THY SELF

By: Dana F. Jokela

Tears of excruciating joy,
Contemplate and then deploy,
Perpetual flow of emotion
Sight of earnest devotion
Waves reiterating, box to drum
Phantasms soon to become
Very quick, almost instantly,
Melded in eternally, thoroughly.
Mended in an empty chest
Vastly filled with zest,
Caused from a heightened decree . . .
That *I love me.*

**HATRED'S TEARS**

By: Robin A. Kephart

Hatred reared its ugly head
one dark and dismal day,
and built a castle on the hill
with cold, dark rooms in which to play.

Her offspring grew in anger,
an evil, wicked seed.
Emotions dead, a heart of stone
and vile words which make souls bleed.

Unleashed upon the world one night
she mingled with the good,
breaking spirits of innocence
and killing those she could.

No rhyme or reason to her game,
No color, sex, or age.
Anyone who journeyed by
was subject to her rage.

Destroying lives she did not know,
running from her fear.
Then one day face to face
she'd meet her reflection in the mirror.

In judgment, she was seated,
claiming a false throne.
Blinded by her sadness
that she carried all alone.

I pity you, dear hatred,
you know not what you've reaped.
A bed of misery you have made
and in it you must sleep.

## YOU ONLY LIVE TO DIE

By: Joey Lynn Brown

You walk the tracks that were left by the souls
that walked this way before,
not knowing what part fate played in their lives.
So you keep traveling on the same road,
one foot in front of the other.
Your confidence made fresh by some kind of pride
because you made it through the day before.
You're not a puppet in a sideshow,
at least you weren't when you were born.
God made each of us as pure as his own Son.
The trades of this world,
that is what makes us dirty,
our souls unclean.
It is up to you to cut the strings of damnation.
You're only free in your mind,
but you can change that with a prayer.
You are free to decide.
So do what you feel is best,
because you only live to die.

## MY MIND IN ITS CURRENT STATE

By: Miko Smith

So much pain in my heart today,
Will I be able to get away?
Pain and misery I have to take,
Just because of a simple mistake.
I'm so sorry for what I have done
I just want to be free, back under the sun.

## CONTEMPLATION

By: Dwight E. Lewis

I was sitting today watching the trees and the grass
Sway gently in a spring breeze . . .
Remembering only a few months ago,
we were in the midst of a deep freeze.
As I sat I pondered the changing of the seasons . . .
And how often in life I went astray for no apparent reason.
So I think to myself on this cloudy yet God-given day . . .
I will go forth on this newly chosen path,
on which I plan to stay.
For as seasons come and then they go . . .
Life can pass me by, and then I'll know:
Did I let opportunity go by me in life?
Like a leaf blowing in the wind?
Or did I seize it and make the most of it
right there and then?
Reflecting back with only my own internal gauge . . .
I see my life and how I've begun to age.
It has been full of adventure and heartaches,
also joy and pain . . .
Yet if I had to live it over again,
I probably wouldn't change a thing.
For this is the life that God gave me
to live and enjoy this day…
And I wouldn't have Him in my heart now,
if I had chosen a different way.

**MY SPIRIT SHALL ALWAYS BE FREE**
By: Frederick D. Howell

My spirit shall always be free.
No man, prison or chains can bind it.
To escape I simply close my eyes,
and I'm free of all confinements,
Sometimes I soar on eagle's wings,
across summer's skies of baby blue.
Or watch the sunrise across a wildflower meadow
that's kissed with morning's dew.
But many times I just go walking,
down some old dusty gravel road,
underneath old oak trees that touch the clouds
where pink wild roses grow.
I can smell their fragrant blossoms now.
Their heavenly scent fills the air,
Or perhaps I'm high on a mountaintop,
with autumn's bright colors everywhere,
At other times I go to grandma's house,
and play beneath her mimosa tree.
A kid once again with my sisters and brothers
laughing together so joyfully free.
Or maybe I'll sit on a snow-covered ridge
with snowflakes falling all around
where red birds and blue jays play
Against nature's pristine white background,
So try as they might,
No man, prison or chains shall ever bind me
For I can always go to the place I love in my mind
My spirit shall always be free . . .

## PLANS FOR THE FUTURE

By: Sammy Butler

Tonight I sit here in my cell, thinking of the past.
Wondering why time has gone by so fast.
I think back to the days when I was a child,
just a carefree kid, out there running wild.
My plans for the future were often shattered
by things of the past that just don't matter.
So to win I cheated, but instead I lost.
So as a loser, I am paying the cost.
I plan for a future I hope will be,
a way of life in which I am free.

# ABOUT TODAY AND TOMORROW IN THEIR OWN WORDS . . .

*The writers give insight into their thoughts about their convictions and their aspirations for the future.*

## The Writers . . .

Dennis E. Anderson
Edward Armstrong
Andre Barfield
Gabriel Bedoya
Duane Anthony Brown
James Butler
Daniel W. Campbell
Kenneth Campbell
Larry D. Cherry
Maurice Coleman
Asa G. A. Collins
Clint Collins
Paul Truman Crowl Jr.
Bernard Dabney
Rodney Edwards
Kevin L. Evans
Raven Everett
Sheldon Gatewood
Allen D. Gentry
Reika E. Hailes
Nathaniel Hamilton
James Ken Harbin
Richard Patrick Horton
Leroy E. Jacobs
Carlton Johnson
Curtis L. Jones
Kevin King
Steven York Lent
Keith Luecke
Johnny Maldonado
Daniel Manning
Randall T. McPheeters
Lee Charles Millsap Jr.
Joseph Modica
Daniel Mullins
Joseph M. Myers
David W. Nelson
Dwayne Stephen Newson
Gregory Ott
Darryl Payne
Darryl Proffit
Rufino Ramirez
Aaron Lamar Sampson
Clayton Sharpe
Gregory J. Shelton
Keith Alan Sherman
Michael Tate
Donald E. Tennyson Jr.
Herman M. Travis
Joe “Rocko” Trevino
Andre Turner
Gregory A. Walker
WM E. H. Wallace
Lester Warfield
Clyde Welch
Rev. Donald A. Wilson Jr.
Joshua A. Wiltfong
Steven Wittman
Joseph Yoder

## Dennis E. Anderson
# 225912

Rape, 15 - 65 years

Never having been involved in our judicial system, it appeared to be fine. After over 11 years of incarceration I remain in disbelief, bewildered by everything. Eternally, I hope to rectify their wrongdoing.

I want to return to academia.

## Edward Armstrong
# 242792

Assault with intent to do great bodily harm
Armed robbery
Felony firearm

I committed my crime using my best thinking. Now I have spent the last nine years incarcerated making my best thinking better so that prison will not be the best I have to offer myself.

I am a scientist. I dedicate my life towards helping to create a world without crime, without war, without insanity, where a man can live his dreams and become successful in his endeavors.

## Andre Barfield
# 99382

Drug charge and possession of a firearm, 7 years

I made a bad choice and I regret it. But, yesterday is gone. I can do nothing about it. But, in Christ Jesus, I have already been forgiven. In him, when I've repented of my mistakes, they no longer exist (Hebrews 10:16). Thank you and may God bless you.

I'm going to go back to school to become an Architect.

## Gabriel Bedoya
# B74853

Wrongly charged, falsely convicted and unjustly incarcerated and punished for surviving a vicious attack. Now I am a former policeman imprisoned with a 30-year sentence.

I plan to aggressively pursue justice, vindication and exoneration and reveal the corruption in the Illinois court system.

## Duane Anthony Brown

# 295-180

Attempted murder
Felonious assault
Aggravated robbery
6 - 25years with gun specification

I took the law into my own hands and tried to take down a drug dealer. I got time, he didn't. I'm coming up on my 8th year in prison.

I hope to watch my seven grandchildren grow into productive adults and try to get a poetry book published.

## James Butler

# 398-298

Burglary, 1 year

I believe I am where I need to be for getting drunk, blacking out, breaking into innocent people's homes and senselessly vandalizing their living rooms.

I want my poetry books published upon my release from prison. I want to sell the many love ballets I have written. I want to invest in real estate and become a millionaire.

## Daniel W. Campbell
# R141-716

Rape (4 counts, 3 victims), life in prison

Rape is a violent criminal act. Soliciting prostitution, even from a minor involves no violence. Incestuous lust that leads to completion of an act of oral sex, even by an eight-or ten-year-old, is immoral, but does not automatically constitute rape. I had consensual sex with my nieces because they were already adept at oral copulation. I was guilty of corruption. I was wrong and I am paying for it with my life.

I hope to be paroled, after 15 years, in January 2002. I hope to return to Kentucky and stay away from televisions and computers. I want to know what normal life is again and enjoy whatever I have left of it. I want to make things, draw things and give things to people who deserve them.

## Kenneth Campbell
# 96392

First-degree murder and robbery
I was sentenced to die on March 26, 1981. I spent 16 years and 3 months on death row and had seven execution dates. On October 27, 1998 my death sentence was changed to life in prison.

Whatever I say, I know that the readers will interpret it through their own personal beliefs (for example, for or against the death penalty). However, I will say that such an unfortunate ordeal, facing a known death, is one not many (thank God) go through. However, I believe that for certain individuals, such as myself, that have been through a furnace of affliction, as gold is purified in fire, can come forth and "shine as gold."

If I should live, I hope to be more aware of each day of life and be more thankful to my God for His gifts that I take too often for granted. Also, I want to be a help and comforter to others, particularly the oppressed and lonely of this world through what I have learned by going through this experience and through the Holy Spirit.

## Larry D. Cherry

# 140540

Carjacking, 8 years

I am guilty as charged. I regret that it happened. It has given me a new perspective into my personality though.

I'd like to explore the world of writing and see where it takes me.

## Maurice Coleman

# 82539

First-degree murder, life in prison

Legally, I am innocent, yet I am unable to prove my innocence without adequate funds to pay for a lawyer to present the injustices of my case. I was railroaded into prison illegally.

I hope to regain my freedom and properly educate the youth. I want to find success and myself a wife to have our children. I'm also presently working on a book of poetry. One day I hope it will be published for the world!

## Asa G. A. Collins
# 508341

Armed robbery and armed criminal action, 20 years.

The question has been asked whether a child who steals is better off being caught and reprimanded or getting away with his offense undetected. This was my first offense of this nature. I have come to appreciate the fact that I did not get away with it, although the stiff sentence imposed is indicative of the inequities of our criminal justice system.

I aspire to be the man I should have liked to have met in my youth, a man whose strength of character would have portrayed the ideal (modern) man. I expect all necessary material things will be subsequently "added unto me."

## Clint Cooper
# 190559

First-degree armed robbery, felony restraint, second-degree assault, 20 years
Class X offender
I've served 16 years flat on a 20-year sentence.

I deserve to do some time, but 16 years is a little too long for the crime. I'm doing as much time or more than a murder and I didn't hurt anyone physically. After 9 years in prison I've come to accept my sentence and have made peace with God and myself.

I aspire to be a successful writer and to use my work to show people (especially Black people) that violence isn't the way. I plan to write a true-to-life account of prison life and the Justice System.

## Paul Truman Crowl Jr.
# 633875

Robbery, 20 years (1992)
I have gotten one half of my sentence done already and I go up again for parole sometime in September.

If I had not been out using drugs I would not be in here. Now that I am here, I am going to do my best to never come back again. I am also sorry for the woman I robbed and wish that someday I could tell her so.

I plan to live one day at a time with the help of the people involved in Narcotics Anonymous and Alcoholics Anonymous and also a God of my understanding.

## Bernard Dabney
# N34409

Felony fraud, 3 years for cashing a check that wasn't mine

I did something wrong, got caught, and was punished for it.

I plan to be the best father I can for my daughter. I'd like to write poems, get back with my daughter's mother and have a pretty good life.

## Rodney Edwards
# B77805

Residential burglary
Aggravated battery
I was given a plea bargain if I plead guilty to the residential burglary act (8 years). The aggravated battery charge was dropped when I took the plea bargain. Now my time is almost over but not soon enough.

I wish I could've done things differently, but no one can turn back the hands of time. All I can do is say I'm sorry for all my past actions that led me astray and ask those who I hurt to believe in me. I always had a good heart. I wouldn't say growing up without that father figure was part of the problem because as a child, we are taught right from wrong. My mother was the greatest father/mother I could've asked for. Since incarcerated, I have attended numerous programs and now this contest is another.

I would love to be in the music business because I am a positive rapper. Also, I'd like to be a poet because a good rapper has to know poetry, speak it, feel it and most of all know what he or she is talking about.

## Kevin L. Evans
# 507819

Second-degree robbery, 12 years (1994)

The criminal justice system ran its own course.

I aspire to be a published author. I have several manuscripts ready for review by a publishing house. I also aspire to own my own business and to be an asset to humanity somehow.

## Raven Everett

# 96616

Murder, life in prison
I've been incarcerated since September 6, 1992.

I have written a program that I really and truly believe will be a worldwide adventure.

## Sheldon Gatewood

# 239344

Armed robbery, 10 - 15 years
Unarmed robbery, 10 - 30 years run concurrently
I have been in prison almost 7 years, since the age of 19.
My first "outdate" is November 2005.

I regret my actions. No one was physically injured and how I wish I could turn back the hands of time. I came to prison as a boy, and have evolved into a man. I am optimistic about life and realize experience is sometimes the wisest and best of teachers. School is now out!

I want to publish my own book of poems, if someone gives me a book deal. I am striving to be a recording artist once I leave prison because I have a positive message to speak.

## Allen D. Gentry

# 339-177

Trafficking and transporting cocaine, 4 - 15 years
I've served more than 4 years back for 28 months on a technical parole violation.

I was not given a fair chance due to my prior history. Basically, I was punished not for the violation but for my original charge. I don't feel that I'll ever leave behind my past to the point that it won't affect my life without some major struggle and sacrifice.

I plan to own my own production company. I will produce, direct and act in my own films. Eventually, I'll make it to the big screen to showcase my talent in front of and behind the scenes.

## Reiko E. Hailes

# 224928

Robbery and malicious wounding, 70 years beginning in 1993

When an individual lacks both parents in a household, he is unaware and uninterested in his or her potential, is without guidance, willpower or determination. When a person lives in poverty, survival is a must. My charges are a result of the way I had to survive in the projects.

I will become famous and wealthy either through a career in Hip-Hop, as a poet, as a clothing designer or as an artist. At least one or more of these scenarios is inevitable.

## Nathaniel Hamilton
# 0163863

3 counts trafficking cocaine and possession,
Transportation and delivery to an undercover agent
I pled not guilty but the court found me guilty and sentenced me to 42 years, mandatory 7 years on each of three 14-year sentences.

I think it was wrong that my cousin was busted selling drugs and just because I was with him 5 or 10 minutes before the incident or the fact that he was giving me a lift home that I was convicted as well. He got busted trying to make a drug deal without my knowledge while I was eating in a restaurant.

My future plans include a job in mechanical engineering, drafting and to be the boss of my own company.

## James Ken Harbin
# 141062

First-degree theft of property, life in prison

I feel that I was sentenced for only one charge and could havc been sentenced for unlawful use of a motor vehicle. I believe a life sentence is too much time for the conviction.

I hope to soon be released form prison and to be able to someday put together a book of poetry and have it published.

## Cory Louis Hines

# 189784

Sale and possession of crack cocaine near a school,
10 years and 7years running concurrently

My future endeavors are to finish my book of exhortations and write my autobiography. I plan to start my own business and enjoy life with my wife and children serving God.

## Richard Patrick Horton

# 367-659

Assault and vandalism

Although I received a lot of time for the crimes I committed, the courts did what they had to do to keep people safe from my temper. I am not mad at the courts for what they did.

I plan to reclaim my business in commercial floor care and become successful and financially independent. I believe I will always write poetry and maybe I'll become famous.

## Leroy E. Jacobs
# 177-399

Rape, 10 - 25 years

A poor man can't get any justice in our court system. Eighteen years of my life taken away so far and I'm no guiltier than the man in the moon!

I plan to be on every computer in Las Vegas, Atlantic City, etc. I am already one of, if not the world's foremost expert on Roulette, or any of the different games, actually.

## Carlton Johnson
# 324-575

Aggravated kidnapping and aggravated robbery, 18 - 50 years

I made some poor decisions in life that led to this term of incarceration. I have learned and realize many things during my imprisonment, primarily about who I am and what I can and want to do upon my release.

I hope to start a software company, deal in real estate investment and become a novelist.

## Curtis L. Jones

# 207927

Drug transportation with intent to distribute, 15years

I lived a life where money ruled because I came up in the streets raising myself. At that time, I thought it was cool to be on top with money. In a sense, the system has me pegged right because some people are out for self. I learned the hard way.

I plan to help handicap kids and to motivate kids to get out of gangs. I want to let them know there is a better way to live. Hopefully, I'll become a great writer someday if God wills it.

## Kevin King

# 171671

Murder (defending myself in a fight), life in prison

The person who testified against me failed three polygraph exams. Shocking!

I plan to seek commendation of sentence and touch my girl every morning. I also plan to get a dog.

## Steven York Lent

# 338-567

Felonious assault, 5 - 15 years
I made parole. My "outdate" is 6-01-2001 after serving 5 years.

I'd like to state my opinion in poetic form:

> We look into the light through eyes of shadow. Walk by way of faith and you'll see peace, liberty and freedom, "The Dream." The only justice is dying, it seems.

To have my poetry book published, entitled, *Chronicles of Cent: Journey through the Mists*, and to become self-sufficient. I want to learn more about Mother Earth and the social impact we have on her as consumers.

## Keith Luecke

# 338-760

Corruption of a minor and child stealing, plea agreement for 8 - 15 years

What I did was inexcusable and I dearly regret my actions. This was my first offense and will definitely be my last.

I have a loving family that has stood by me and my future plans are to be with them. I plan to support them and prove that their trust was not misplaced.

## Johnny Maldonado

# 2744441-M353

I want to be with the lady I love, and maybe, start a family. Of course, I plan to keep writing and working.

## Daniel Manning
# 116831

I was initially charged with capital murder, which was reduced to first-degree murder. Sentence: life imprisonment (with a plea bargain)

My counsel, a court-appointed attorney lied to me. I was under the impression, since my lawyer told me, that I would only do about 12 to 15 years. Yes, a man died, and yes, by my actions, yet there were circumstances surrounding this incident. It was not pre-meditated which is what first-degree murder means. I was misled and my public defender was not to be trusted.

I hope for clemency. Perhaps, I'll show someone some of my works as a writer/poet. I'll hopefully, publish my work and let people other than just the population here in prison see and read my work. My writing is dark and has a lonely, soulful impact. Basically, that's how I feel most of everyday. I want to release my inner feelings. Depression is hard to handle. My aspiration is to keep my sanity by venting i.e., writing.

## Randall T. McPheeters
# 114037

2 counts of first-degree murder, 2 life sentences

I want to write novels and be free one day.

## Lee Charles Millsap Jr.

# 113121

Capital murder, life in prison without parole

I admit to committing the murder, but I believe the charge and sentence is too much. I believe the state neglected to look at the fact that it was my first time, and they basically wanted the biggest conviction they could pin on me by any means.

I expect to prove an injustice in the courts and start over again. I will then continue to succeed.

## Joseph Modica

# 363129

I was charged with stealing a credit card.

Basically, I am an addict, and instead of working on fixing the problem I dove deeper into it. In doing so, I had to steal to support my habit. I guess it was a blessing to get caught. Now, I can stop the insanity and work on my recovery.

I plan to go back to school and get a Masters in Adolescent Psychology. I would like to be a counselor for a high school. I feel I can relate with teens and can help them to make positive choices.

## Daniel Mullins

# 152385

I do not want any information pertaining to my crime disclosed.

I plan to continue fighting my case, stay healthy and return to society.

## Joseph M. Myers
# R143-651

I hope to someday continue in the Graphic Arts field as well as continue my writing. I plan to attend the Joe Kubert School of Cartoon and Graphic Arts.

## David W. Nelson
# 0299882

First-degree burglary, 30 years
Attempted second-degree rape, 20 years

I have acquired new information about my case in which a prominent government agency in North Carolina has reported in a different analysis of the DNA that I'm not the one who committed the crime. My attorney is working to get me a new trial since the information that would have exonerated me was not used in my trial.

I hope to be released from prison and to prove that the judicial system is not for people who are poor. I want to start my life over without the law trying to pin any crime on me without physical evidence and to take care of my mother who stood by me no matter what the circumstances were and encouraged me to fulfill my dreams.

## Dwayne Stephen Newson
# A310-275

Rape, life in prison

The real crime is being innocent of a crime and not being given a fair trial due to a lack of finances. I was forced to pick a card to decide my fate and told by the judge to, "Give God a try."

I plan to publish one of my finished books of poetry and short stories for children. Once I am free I will write my soul.

## Gregory A. Ott
# 282372

Murder, life in prison

I plan to secure parole, attempt to see my parents and live quietly ever after.

## Darryl Payne
# 78921

Voluntary manslaughter, 1 - 20 years
Aggravated assault, 1 - 7 years
Malicious destruction of property, 1 - 5 years
Total, 3 - 32 years

I was raised to believe that people should admit when they are wrong and suffer the consequences of their choices. I am, therefore, suffering the consequences of my choices.

I am considering writing and motivational speaking as sources of income. For my own satisfaction, I would like PhDs in Political Science and African-American History.

## Darryl Proffit
# 222938

While on parole, I committed a bank robbery in Adrian, Michigan. I was offered a plea- bargain of 7 1/2 - 20 years along with good time. I am eligible for community placement by July 2003.

Wrong is wrong, period. It was strictly bad judgment and I had no right to commit this crime whatsoever. I take it as a lesson learned; no one can take something bad and expect something good out of it. I will make this the transition point in making myself a better person.

I plan to get my life together so that I may inspire someone who is less fortunate than I. With God's help, I may one day have the chance to write my autobiography and own my own business.

## Rufino Ramirez
# L17554

2 counts of burglary,
2 counts of grand theft
1 count of dealing in stolen property
I was sentenced to 48 months in a federal state prison.

I'm appealing my sentence because I was illegally sentenced.

I plan to raise my daughter and go on to become a boxer!

## Aaron Lamar Sampson
# B79038

Aggravated robbery, 10 years

I feel I have been given the chance to gain control of my life as well as be a better parent to my children.

I hope to have my recently completed novel entitled, *Willie's Book: Lama Sabachthani*, published. Hopefully, one day it'll be a bestseller. I'd like to write more books.

## Clayton Sharpe

# 190785

Forgery

I paid for that misjudgment.

I plan to go as far as my mind will take me.

## Gregory J. Shelton

# 711643

Delivering cocaine, 25 years

Gosh what a killer question! I guess, what I really wanted was enough money to buy some land and a home and start some type of business.

I plan to get my life back on track and live an honest and successful life. Also, I hope to one day own my own business.

## Keith Alan Sherman

# 366598

Rape, 9 years and 5 years post-release control, "outdate" Sept 8, 2007.

I was sexually abused all my life. I can't remember life without sex. That's no excuse for what I did. After I was convicted that didn't matter, I was the monster. And I was. I never hurt anyone physically, but mentally, yes. Anyway, I was left all alone until I met Christ. He has forgiven me and comforts me. That's what my poem was about, "A True Friend" that won't leave you for mistakes or anything. Amen.

I plan to get into some type of ministry for the Lord to help prevent sexual abuse and to show people where true happiness and joy is, in Christ, not sex or drugs or alcohol. I searched for 40 years for something to take the guilt and hurt away and I finally found it, Christ. Amen.

## Michael Tate

# 1001236

Forgery, 8 years

My opinion is that I got what I deserved. I've learned a lot since then and I'm making my life better. There is more to life than taking advantage of people.

My future dreams are to teach young adults that prison is not a fun place to live. There is more to life than crime. Pick up a book and explore your mind.

## Donald E. Tennyson Jr.

# 347-222

Rape, 9 - 25 years of which I have done 5 years.

I committed the crime for which I am now being punished. My opinion on the matter is that I am guilty. Words cannot express the profound nature of this experience. I am truly sorry for what I did; however, to have one's freedom suddenly taken tends to overshadow all but the extreme guilt of one's actions.

My aspiration is that of all incarcerated men, to be remembered for something better than my last un-incarcerated action. I would like to have a career in writing, maybe work on a screenplay or two.

## Herman M. Travis

# 351-557

Aggravated burglary, weapon under disability and shooting into a habitat/school. I was sentenced to 5 years with mandatory 3 years (gun specification to be served). My first release date is July 2002.

Once, I was blind to the love and devotion that I had from a family and didn't share in that love. My eyes have been opened to that love since my incarceration. I see two different interpretations: in my wrongdoing, I was made right. My sins will be forgiven and in time my pain will subside from the brightness I see since my blindfold has been removed.

I want to continue writing for others who may feel the way I do yet cannot form the words. I hope to change the myth of "once this, always this." A man can change if he truly wants to. I want to be a spokesperson for anyone who has felt alone or abandoned in life. In being left alone, we find ourselves.

## Joe "Rocko" Trevino
# 920949

Prohibited weapon and attempted burglary, 8 years

When I committed these crimes I was 18. I did 7 years of probation on an 8-year deferred adjudicated sentence. I got revoked on the probation in the last year because of a misdemeanor. I am now serving 8 years. I feel like the justice system has failed to honor a patriotic citizen.

I plan to help my children achieve their goals. I hope to find peace within myself and share it with others. I plan to find prosperity and share it with others who seek harmony in life.

## Andre Turner
# K71901

Vehicular hijacking, 4 years
2 counts of forgery, 2 years for each count run concurrently
I have a 6-year sentence, leaving me with an "outdate" of 9-25-02.

Well, I want to begin by admitting that I did break the law. Yes, I did make some bad choices. I've made mistakes. People see me and visualize me as a failure; but they're wrong. So, my opinion on the matter is that I did a crime that I'm paying for with days I can never get back. Basically, what I'm saying is, there have been times that I became a victim of circumstance.

First, while I'm here I plan to reorganize my thoughts. Secondly, once I'm released, I plan to make common sense my best friend. But, most importantly, I plan to work hard to become a bone and skin specialist to help people with the common disease, Lupus, which burdens my mother. I'm simply searching for a future with real luminosity to it.

## Gregory A. Walker
# 386-378

1 count burglary, 8 years (7 remaining)

I was unjustly convicted.
The hope of my conviction being reversed is still alive.

I look forward to being reunited with my only son, 8-year-old Alex. I plan to embark on a spiritual odyssey and continue writing poetry.

## WM E. H. Wallace
# 250-485

Rape, 15-150 years

I've taken responsibility for the things I'm guilty of. I've learn to accept, deal with and get rid of the anger I once had for the things I was falsely accused of. Finally, I've learned the skills I need not to repeat the mistakes I made that put me behind bars.

Upon release, I plan to apply for Electrical Certification and do residential and commercial wiring. I may start a business of my own and continue with my hobbies, especially, writing and playing piano.

## Lester Warfield

# N64454

Armed robbery, home invasion, first-degree attempted murder, unlawful restraint, 8 years. Also, I was charged with aggravated battery and unlawful possession of a weapon since being incarcerated for which I've received an additional 7 years.

No one is beyond mistakes when ignorance is his companion.

I plan to do all I need to do along reasonable lines to remain on a positive path. Also, I hope to become one with a very special woman I've encountered since I've been incarcerated. It is she who inspires me to stay focused.

## Clyde Welch

# 237-500

Assault
Attempted Rape

I wasn't in my right mind while using drugs and booze. It's something that never should have happened.

I plan to try and make things right and go on with my life. I'm a much-improved person now.

## Rev. Donald A. Wilson Jr.

# 240199

Drug charge, 7 - 20 years
I'm doing flat time for my first offense.

I was wrong for what I did and I hope to get a second chance to show that I can also be a productive citizen in this world.

I plan to work and be productive in life and spend time with my loved ones.

## Joshua A. Wiltfong

# 289407

Carrying a concealed weapon, 2 - 5 years.

It was probably best that I was stopped before I reached my destination.

I hope to move home and start a new life with my fiancée, Danielle B. Osborne.

## Steven Wittman

# 292697

Possession of a controlled substance and driving while intoxicated, 3 years

I accept full responsibility for my incarceration. I was given several chances and blew them all. The puzzling question is: why is alcohol, the most dangerous and socially devastating drug, the only one that is legal? Alcohol has caused me twice the grief heroin ever did.

I am currently working on a hybrid novel; let's say Ann Rice and Kurt Vonnegut. I wish to finish that work and get it published. I would also like to get out.

## Joseph Yoder

# 317263

2 counts armed robberies, home invasion and felony firearms, 11 – 32 years
I took a plea bargain for the home invasion and felony firearms charges.
I am up for parole in 2011.

Of course, I feel angry and sad. I had to be separated from my son who I was raising by myself. My mother has him now. I didn't do what I did for money. I had been fighting with the people whose house I went in for a while. They kept calling and harassing my mother. One night they called and threatened to rape her, so I did what I did.

I am currently writing two books. I write raps constantly and have over 100 verses memorized. I'm also in a horticulture class. I like working outdoors. I want to work with nature, animals and plants someday as well as work on my writing and rapping careers.

**Special thanks to all correctional institutions that actively participated, especially the following:**

Augusta Correctional Institution
Bedford Hills Correctional Facility
Belmont Correctional Institution
Brevard Correctional Institution
Brown Creek Correctional Institution
Central Missouri Correctional Center
Chillicothe Correctional Institution
Chippewa Correctional Facility
Columbia River Correctional Institution
Coxsackie Correctional Facility
Cummins Unit
Deep Meadow Correctional Center
Darrington Correctional Facility
Morgan County Regional Correctional
NECC
Oregon Department of Correctional Facility